W9-BFE-911

THE COLLABORATIVE WAY TO DIVORCE

STUART G. WEBB invented Collaborative law in 1990 and has practiced exclusively in the Collaborative method ever since. He trains and lectures throughout North America and Europe. He has appeared on *CBS Evening News* and in the *New York Times* and *Wall Street Journal.* In 2002 Mr. Webb was the corecipient of the American Bar Association's First Annual Lawyer as Problem Solver Award. Stu lives in Minneapolis, Minnesota, with his wife, Martha.

RON D. OUSKY is a Collaborative attorney and a worldwide leader in the Collaborative movement. He was one of the pioneers of the Collaborative method and is on the board of the International Academy of Collaborative Professionals (IACP). Ron is a frequent speaker and writer on Collaborative practice and has appeared on network television. He lives in Edina, Minnesota, with his wife, Marlys, and their three children, Maria, Dano, and Katie.

Writing this book has been a labor of love. If you'd like to share your experiences with using this book, or with the Collaborative practice, e-mail the authors at stuwbb@aol.com and ron@ousky.com.

THE
COLLABORATIVE
WAY TO DIVORCE

The Revolutionary Method
That Results in Less Stress,
Lower Costs, and Happier Kids—
WITHOUT GOING TO COURT

STUART G. WEBB
FOUNDER, COLLABORATIVE DIVORCE LAW,
AND RON D. OUSKY

Ⓟ

A PLUME BOOK

PLUME
Published by Penguin Group
Penguin Group (USA) Inc., 375 Hudson Street, New York, New York 10014, U.S.A.
Penguin Group (Canada), 90 Eglinton Avenue East, Suite 700, Toronto, Ontario, Canada
M4P 2Y3 (a division of Pearson Penguin Canada Inc.)
Penguin Books Ltd., 80 Strand, London WC2R 0RL, England
Penguin Ireland, 25 St. Stephen's Green, Dublin 2, Ireland (a division of Penguin Books Ltd.)
Penguin Group (Australia), 250 Camberwell Road, Camberwell, Victoria 3124, Australia
(a division of Pearson Australia Group Pty. Ltd.)
Penguin Books India Pvt. Ltd., 11 Community Centre,
Panchsheel Park, New Delhi – 110 017, India
Penguin Group (NZ), 67 Apollo Drive, Rosedale, North Shore 0745, Auckland, New Zealand
(a division of Pearson New Zealand Ltd.)
Penguin Books (South Africa) (Pty.) Ltd., 24 Sturdee Avenue, Rosebank,
Johannesburg 2196, South Africa

Penguin Books Ltd., Registered Offices: 80 Strand, London WC2R 0RL, England

Published by Plume, a member of Penguin Group (USA) Inc. Previously published in a Hudson Street Press Edition

First Plume Printing, July 2007
10 9 8 7 6 5 4 3 2 1

℗ REGISTERED TRADEMARK—MARCA REGISTRADA

The Library of Congress has catalogued the Hudson Street Press edition as follows:
Webb, Stuart G.
    The collaborative way to divorce : the revolutionary method that results in less stress,
lower costs, and happier kids, without going to court / Stuart G. Webb and Ron Ousky.
        p. cm.
    ISBN 1-59463-022-4 (hc.)
    ISBN 978-0-452-28835-5 (pbk.)
    1. Divorce suits—United States—Popular works. 2. Compromise (Law)—United
States—Popular works. 3. Dispute resolution (Law)—United States—Popular works. 4.
Attorney and client—United States—Popular works. I. Ousky, Ron. II. Title.
KF535.Z9W35 2006
346.7301'66—dc22

                                                                        2006005150

Printed in the United States of America

PUBLISHER'S NOTE
This publication is designed to provide accurate and authoritative information in regard to the
subject matter covered. It is sold with the understanding that the publisher is not engaged in
rendering legal, accounting or other professional services. If you require legal advice or other
expert assistance, you should seek the services of a competent professional.

To our wives, Martha and Marlys

ACKNOWLEDGMENTS

We would like to thank all of the people who have contributed to this book through their ideas and encouragement.

We particularly want to acknowledge all of our clients who have had the courage and wisdom to see that divorce is not just a crisis, but an opportunity to look within themselves to meet the important challenges that lie ahead of them. We'd also like to thank the Collaborative practitioners around the world for making lives better for clients and families—and themselves. We are especially grateful for our colleagues at the Collaborative Law Institute of Minnesota, who have helped us so much in our community, and the leaders and members of the IACP who have done so much to make the Collaborative option available to families around the world. There are so many wonderful pioneers in this movement that we find ourselves learning something new every time we get together.

We also wish to thank our agent, Jim Levine, who has helped us stay focused during this great adventure, as well as Armin Brott, who helped us make this book more clear.

And finally, we want to thank Laureen Rowland, founder and publisher of Hudson Street Press, for having the vision to see how a book about Collaborative divorce will make a difference in the lives of many families. In addition to being the person who truly made this book happen, Laureen has provided invaluable guidance that greatly improved the tone and content of the book.

On a more personal level, each of us would like to thank the following people.

Stu

I want to thank my wife, Martha, who provides a stable presence in support of peace and collaboration.

My grown children—Kim, Lisa, and Craig—are an inspiration, as are my five grandchildren—Libby, Tori, Trevor, Nicholas, and Tyler.

My sister, Sally, has always been a supporting presence.

And my ancestors would never forgive me if I didn't sincerely honor my small-town upbringing in Rolfe, Iowa.

Ron

I want to thank the following people:

My wife and my best friend, Marlys, who has stood by me through these twenty-six years and supported my dreams.

My three wonderful children—Maria, Dano, and Katie—who bring endless joy into my life and who help me appreciate the great miracle of parenthood.

My mother, who encouraged me to build castles in the air.

My father, who taught me much about true humility.

My siblings—Rich, Terry, Diane, and Rene—for being with me through every step of my journey.

The many friends who have supported my work, particularly

Mick Cochrane and Stephen Cohen, two great friends and writers who helped me find my voice.

My colleague, Amy Jensen Wolff, for making the Collaborative Alliance dream come true.

The people of Milroy, Minnesota, for giving me a special place to grow up.

CONTENTS

INTRODUCTION

Every thirty-two seconds, a child in America witnesses his or her parent's divorce. And while divorce, even under the best circumstances, is marked by a range of emotions (disappointment, anger, hurt, betrayal, sadness, fear, and loss, to name just a few), research now reveals that *how* a couple conducts themselves during a divorce has far greater impact on their children than the act of divorcing itself.

Offering a dignified, effective, and highly strategic solution to one of life's most difficult and emotionally charged situations, this book presents a completely new way—a smarter way—to get divorced. It's called the Collaborative method of divorce, and simply put, it means that you, your spouse, and both of your lawyers agree to focus your efforts on civilly dissolving your marriage and dividing your assets, with no intention of ever going to court. While Collaborative divorce is similar to mediation in that both parties focus on finding common interests, rather than finding reasons to attack each other and defend their respective positions, Collaborative divorce goes well beyond mediation. Rather than employing a neutral party (mediator) who cannot offer advice or opinions, the Collaborative process allows each person in the couple to hire active legal representation. Stressing cooperation over confrontation and resolution over revenge, the smart divorce is both highly strategic and beneficial in that: It gives the couple greater control over the outcome of their divorce; resolution is generally less expensive and quicker than going to court; it benefits the children by keeping them out of the controversy; and it helps the couple to maintain a sense of integrity and respect, which is often a priority when children are involved.

While this may *sound* simple enough, in reality it's a radical and revolutionary agreement for divorcing couples and their attorneys to make.

The majority of couples who go through the Collaborative method come through the process satisfied with the results. And more importantly, they are able to avoid the lingering hostility and anger that are so common among divorced couples and they stand a good chance of preserving what's still positive in their relationship and their relationships with their children. It's no wonder we call it the smart divorce!

So how and why did this process develop, and why has it caught on so dramatically throughout the United States, Canada, and an increasing number of other countries worldwide? We'll get to that in a minute. But first, let us tell you a little about us.

The Collaborative Way to Divorce is written by two attorneys who work exclusively with this Collaborative model—Stuart Webb, who originated the Collaborative method of divorce, and Ron Ousky, a pioneer of the process.

Stu's Story

In 1989, I had been a divorce lawyer for about eighteen years—and was getting pretty sick of it. I saw what the adversarial court battles that were the focus of divorce were doing to my clients, and I knew the resulting negativity was having an effect on me, too.

In traditional litigation two lawyers (or teams of lawyers) hash out the divorce in a court of law. The actual parties to the divorce—the husband and wife—have almost no direct contact with each other, and what little interaction they have is usually bitter and unproductive. Tension, fear, anger, and recrimination prevail. This traditional process makes it almost impossible for the parties to have anything remotely resembling a healthy relationship after the divorce, even when there are children involved.

As a divorce litigator, I'd felt for a long time that I was living in a siege mentality, merely waiting for the next battle to start, and finally I got to the point where I was ready to quit the practice of law. I enrolled in a college and was ready to start educating myself for a new career when I had one last thought about practicing law:

"If I'm actually willing to quit being a lawyer, why don't I at least see whether there's some out-of-the-box way I can look at things. Maybe there's a better way of handling divorce."

So I began experimenting with different ways to approach family law practice. In late 1989, I was involved in one of the worst litigation cases of my career, a real showcase of everything that's wrong with litigation (lying, nasty tricks, hiding assets, endless court hearings, and so on). That case in and of itself could have been enough to get me to retire. But in the midst of one of those awful hearings, it occurred to me that there should be settlement-only specialists available for divorcing couples, specialists who work with the couple outside the court system, and who would turn the case over to trial lawyers if and only if the settlement process failed.

That, in a nutshell, was the birth of Collaborative law.

On January 1, 1990, I declared myself a Collaborative lawyer—the first, and only, one. I knew, though, that Collaborative law could never succeed if I were the only one doing it. So I mentioned the concept to some other local divorce lawyers, and by the end of 1990 there were nine of us.

One of the attorneys who joined the Collaborative movement during those early stages was Ron Ousky, who became my colleague, my friend, and the coauthor on this book. I'll let Ron tell you about himself.

Meet Ron

I chose to practice divorce law because I thought I could make a difference for families in conflict. During the early part of my career I thought that meant protecting my clients or trying to save them by "winning" in court. As the years progressed, however, it became increasingly evident that even when my client "won," his or her financial and emotional life was often left in a shambles. I started feeling like a bull in a china shop, unable to accomplish anything of real value without creating significant damage.

I became convinced that there had to be a better way to practice family law, a way that wasn't so damaging to families. In the early 1990s, I heard that Stu Webb, a lawyer I'd opposed in a traditional divorce case, had developed a family court alternative that he was calling Collaborative law. I took Stu's first training and eventually joined his Collaborative Law Institute.

I handled a few Collaborative cases during those early years, but didn't completely grasp just how this method would ultimately change the way that divorce is practiced. I was afraid that our system was so entrenched in the adversarial way of doing things that the Collaborative method wouldn't stand a chance.

But in early 2000, I started looking at Collaborative law more optimistically. Stu Webb's "little idea" had spread from Minneapolis to various other parts of the country, and now hundreds of attorneys were using the Collaborative method and practicing throughout North America. What amazed me most of all was that the idea had spread simply by word of mouth, with no attempt on Stu's part to really market the idea.

This remarkable growth was being driven by clients and lawyers who had come to understand that the Collaborative method offers a whole new way of resolving the complex issues involved in family conflicts.

Clearly, I couldn't sit on the sidelines anymore. I jumped in with both feet, and I soon became one of the leaders in the international effort to help clients around the world understand the benefits of the Collaborative process.

As the Collaborative divorce movement grew steadily over the years, local, national, and international media such as the *CBS Evening News*, the *New York Times*, the *Wall Street Journal, Chicago Tribune*, and the *Christian Science Monitor* began to take note. And of course the idea caught on in the legal community as well. We estimate that today there are eight to ten thousand Collaborative lawyers spanning forty states and all of Canada, reaching into the United Kingdom, Australia, and several other countries as well.

It was clear to us—two of the pioneers of the Collaborative movement—that we were rapidly approaching a "tipping point," and that our so-called radical approach realistically could become the predominant method of handling divorce.

Why This Book?

Since its humble beginnings in 1990, Collaborative law has helped thousands of couples achieve better results and create better lives for themselves and their children. But despite the momentum behind the movement and the media coverage, most couples who file for divorce are still unaware of the Collaborative option. Also, while many books and articles have been written to teach professionals about this method, there is nothing available to help you, the reader, understand the benefits of the Collaborative process and how it works.

The Collaborative Way to Divorce is designed to address both of these issues. Guiding you through the steps of the Collaborative process so that you may make better, more informed decisions in order to meet your goals, *The Collaborative Way to Divorce* isn't about "going easy" on your spouse. It's about getting what you want while ending up with less expense, less stress, and happier kids, without going to court.

How This Book Is Organized

In Part One, we provide an overview of how the traditional divorce process works as compared to the Collaborative method. We'll also talk about some of the other nontraditional divorce options out there and help you evaluate which option is best for you and your family.

In Part Two, we shift our focus to include others who are essential to the success of your Collaborative divorce. We'll show you ways to enroll your spouse in the Collaborative process so that you both can prepare to work toward your many common goals, how to select Collaborative attorneys, and how to identify the other professionals (such as accountants, therapists, and coaches) who can help you along the way.

In Part Three, we provide a more in-depth understanding of the Collaborative process. We begin with a discussion of Collaborative four-way meetings, and explore how the Collaborative process works in relation to some very specific issues you might be concerned about, such as possession of your home, determining parenting time, and financial support obligations. In this section we also walk you through the three basic steps that will determine the success of your Collaborative journey.

Finally, in Part Four, we explain each phase of the Collaborative process, from the first four-way meeting through completion of the divorce proceedings.

Throughout *The Collaborative Way to Divorce* we illustrate many important points by introducing you to hypotheticals and to some of our clients (whose names and identities have been changed, of course) and their specific situations. We have also prepared a lengthy appendix, complete with forms, summaries, and a wide variety of tools to provide you with everything you need to reach a successful, smarter outcome in your Collaborative divorce.

By the end of this book, we hope that you will have decided to join the growing number of divorcing couples who have used the Collaborative method to protect the people and things that matter most in their lives.

PART ONE

Making the Right Decision:

How Collaborative Divorce Differs from Other Approaches

CHAPTER 1

The Basics:

Comparing the Collaborative Process to a Traditional Divorce

Preparing for a divorce can be a confusing, bewildering, and often frightening experience. In a lot of ways it's like preparing to take a trip to a strange country, a place you've never been to, a place where the conditions are harsh and the customs and language are completely unknown to you.

As with any trip, it's essential to know where you want to end up before you plot out your itinerary. The same applies to your divorce. Where do you want to be emotionally, physically, and psychologically after it's over? How do you want your life to look? We're assuming that you have a pretty good idea. If not, we suggest that before reading any further you take a break and spend some time thinking about the direction you want your life to take. Talk to a trusted friend or, better yet, spend some time alone jotting down your wishes and dreams on paper or in a journal. You may be surprised to learn how much of this is close to the surface, even if you've not yet taken the time to articulate it.

A little later in this book, we'll take a look at your big-picture plan to make sure that you've carefully considered the most important issues. But for now, here's a preview of the journey you're about to undertake.

*   *   *

There are, of course, many different ways to get from one place to another. There are easy ways and hard ways. While we can't promise that this book will make your divorce easy, we know from helping hundreds of clients that the Collaborative process will make it a lot less painful.

To help make your journey more manageable, we've broken down the entire divorce process into eight basic stages. In this chapter, we'll briefly describe how each of the stages works in a traditional divorce process. We'll point out some of the problems with the traditional model and we'll explain how the Collaborative method offers a far better alternative.

Everyone's divorce situation is a little different, but we've found that most of the clients we work with go through these stages in the following order:

1. Finding and hiring an attorney
2. Starting the divorce process
3. Addressing temporary issues
4. Gathering and exchanging information
5. Hiring experts
6. Negotiating a settlement
7. Getting a "final" divorce decree
8. Resolving issues that arise after the divorce

Step One: Finding and Hiring an Attorney

For most people facing divorce, the first step is to find an attorney who can guide you through the process. Like a good travel guide, he or she has led many people along the same path, knows the terrain, knows the language and the customs, and can be a great resource in helping you reach your destination safely.

The success of your journey may depend a great deal on finding an attorney who is a good fit for you and who has the skills and experience to guide you toward your goals in the most effective way.

The Traditional Method: Fighting Fire with Fire

Since it's considered unethical for one attorney to represent both parties in a divorce, you and your spouse will each need to choose your own. In the traditional divorce process, the two of you would conduct separate searches. You'd ask friends and relatives for recommendations, read some books or magazine articles about how to select an attorney, and maybe do some research on the Internet. Most of these resources would encourage you to protect yourself by hiring an attorney who is "a great litigator" or "good in court."

Worrying that your spouse is looking for a tough, aggressive attorney, you'd try to find someone even tougher (that's just human nature!). After all, you have to fight fire with fire. So even if you'd really prefer to work things out civilly, you'd still opt for an aggressive lawyer out of fear that a "settlement lawyer" would get eaten alive by your spouse's hard-nosed litigator, and you'd be left destitute.

Your spouse, of course, is going through exactly the same exercise—whether she likes it or not.

Disadvantages of the Traditional Method

As you can probably foresee, there are some significant problems with the traditional approach. First, there's a good chance that as a result of all the second-guessing you and your spouse are doing, neither of you will end up with the kind of representation you actually want and need. It's definitely a lose-lose situation.

Second, although some people can benefit from working with an aggressive lawyer, the overwhelming majority don't. Less than 5 percent of all divorce cases actually go to trial. The rest settle before they ever get to court. So while you're out looking for courtroom pizzazz, you've likely overlooked a much more important qualification: negotiating skills. Hiring an aggressive attorney is a little like hiring a contractor to build your house based on his or her reputation as a demolitions expert.

Third, if you and your spouse do end up choosing attorneys with radically different philosophies, your chances of reaching any kind of reasonable settlement are limited, which can only mean court, with all of its accompanying stresses and expenses, whether you like it or not.

An Alternative: The Collaborative Method

In the Collaborative process, you and your spouse *coordinate* your search for attorneys. More specifically, you both agree to hire attorneys who are trained in settling cases through Collaborative strategies. Since Collaborative attorneys share the same philosophy and training, neither you nor your spouse will experience the fear factor that might otherwise prompt you to hire an overly aggressive attorney. In short, you both get what you want.

Collaborative attorneys actually sign a contract that commits them—along with you and your spouse—to reaching a settlement. The contract, called a Participation Agreement, requires the attorneys to withdraw from your case if they can't resolve all of your issues out of court. This ability to bind both attorneys in this manner is what makes the Collaborative process different from any other method.

"My wife and I both wanted to settle our issues out of court so that our children wouldn't get caught in the middle. But my wife doesn't trust me and thought she'd have to get an aggressive attorney to protect her rights. I gave her some information about Collaborative divorce and she agreed to meet with a Collaborative attorney to find out about the process. Meeting with the attorney helped my wife realize that she could protect her rights *without* having to go to court."

—Sam B.

Many of our clients have asked why they can't keep their Collaborative lawyers if the collaboration breaks down. The answer is that the agreement to withdraw is what makes the Collaborative process work. Why? Traditionally, attorneys have been trained in law schools and in daily trial practice to take charge of your case, make positional arguments (no matter how unsound), and prepare your case for trial. Even if you and your husband or wife really want to work things out amicably, there can be a seeming tendency toward going to court from the mere inclinations of the lawyers. So, if you want to emphasize settlement, you'll need a new breed of lawyer, someone who is specially trained to work in a client-centered settlement context. To make that work, the agreement that all efforts are made for settlement outside of court needs to be in place.

If your Collaborative lawyers have exhausted every option and can't achieve resolution (which happens in less than 10 percent of cases), the settlement phase ends and you turn to litigation and trial lawyers.

If you're skeptical about your ability to convince your spouse to hire a Collaborative attorney, you aren't alone. The emotions that precede a divorce often lead people to believe that clear, mutually beneficial communication is impossible. But, having personally worked with hundreds of divorcing couples, we've seen that convincing the other spouse isn't as difficult as most people imagine, as long as certain important steps are taken very early in the process. We'll outline those steps in chapter 3.

Finding a Collaborative Attorney

Only a decade ago, finding a skilled Collaborative attorney was a challenge. But the number of attorneys adopting the Collaborative approach has been nearly doubling every year for the past several years, making it increasingly easy to find a Collaborative attorney near you. The International Academy of Collaborative Professionals (www.Collaborative practice.com) lists Collaborative law practice groups and individuals in almost every state in the United States and almost every province in Canada, and in several other countries as well. In most instances you will be able to read detailed information about each attorney, including the amount of Collaborative training he or she has had, other specialized training, general experience, and education. We'll talk about how to find a Collaborative attorney later in the book.

Step Two: Starting the Divorce Process

There is an old Chinese proverb that says that "a journey of a thousand miles begins with a single step." Taking that first step can be terrifying, but once it's done, a lot of the pressure will be relieved and the rest of the process will seem less intimidating. But *how* you take that first step and the direction in which you decide to go is critical because it sets the tone for everything else that follows.

The Traditional Method: Papers Are Served

A traditional divorce typically starts when you or your spouse prepares (usually with the assistance of an attorney) a Summons and Petition. A Summons is an official court document that commands your spouse to do certain things, including submitting an official Answer to your Petition. A Petition is a court document that states certain facts in your case and outlines what you want from your spouse or the court.

The Summons and Petition are served on (meaning hand delivered to) your spouse. They are filed at your local courthouse so that the court (and the public) are made aware of your request for a divorce.

Once the papers are served, your spouse must prepare an Answer and Counter-Petition, a formal document that states what your spouse wants in the divorce process. These papers are also filed with the court.

Once all the documents have been filed, a judge is generally assigned to your case. At that point, depending on where you live, the court may then determine how your case will proceed on the court calendar.

Disadvantages of the Traditional Method

Preparing, serving, and filing the Summons and Petition and the Answer and Counter-Petition can cost both you and your spouse hundreds of dollars—money that you either could have deferred or avoided altogether.

More importantly, starting a divorce in this formal way is often seen as a hostile or adversarial act. And the embarrassment and shock felt by the one who receives the initial papers may trigger an even more aggressive response. As a result, you and your spouse suddenly may find yourselves heading in a direction neither of you expected or wanted to go, well before either one of you has had the opportunity to fully consider your options.

Lisa and George had a very quiet marriage. Some might have argued that it was too quiet. But George never thought so. He never liked to go out that much anyway, and he enjoyed relaxing at home after work, listening to music and reading to the kids.

Lisa recently went to visit her mother for a week, and one evening when she was away, there was a knock on the door. When George answered it, he found himself face-to-face with a process server who handed him two official-looking documents, a Summons and a Petition. Reading through them, George discovered that Lisa was asking for a divorce and was seeking, among other things, custody of the children, child support, spousal maintenance, equitable division of the parties' property, and title to their home. According to the documents, George had thirty days to respond legally or Lisa could get everything she was requesting. In addition, George actually didn't even have thirty days—another document, a Notice of Temporary Hearing, informed him that in three weeks Lisa would be going to court and asking for an order to remove George from the house.

Shocked and afraid and unable to discuss both his feelings and these papers with Lisa, George spent a restless night. In the morning he sought out the best adversarial lawyer he could find. The litigation lines were drawn and both parties and their attorneys began preparing documentation for the temporary hearing—the first round in a long series of adversarial proceedings.

While there are certainly cases where this approach is necessary, it's important to carefully consider all of the implications before making a choice that may cause irreparable harm—to yourself, your spouse, or the resolution process. Theoretically it's possible to shift gears and pursue a different strategy even after serving the Summons and Petition. But it's not easy. The sting of rejection, humiliation, embarrassment, or shame each of you feels may make it difficult to consider a full range of settlement options with a cool head.

The View from Both Sides

"My wife told me that she didn't want a nasty divorce. I assumed that meant she would prepare some kind of settlement offer. The next thing I know a process server shows up at my office and serves me divorce papers. After being embarrassed in front of my coworkers, I pretty much decided my wife couldn't be trusted, and I hired the most aggressive attorney I could find. Our divorce was hard fought from beginning to end and we spent tens of thousands of dollars in unnecessary legal fees."

—Ralph S.

"I really believe my husband and I could have worked out many of the issues on our own. When I met with an attorney to get the divorce process going, he told me that some of the papers would have to be served on my husband, that that was the standard way of doing things. But my husband was furious at the way it was handled. He called me immediately afterward to tell me that he was going to hire a 'barracuda' to represent him. After that, we were never able to sit down and talk without the attorneys around. We ended up having the expensive, nasty divorce I had thought we could avoid."

—Rita S.

An Alternative: The Collaborative Method of Starting a Divorce

In the Collaborative method, most of the formal steps outlined above are either waived or postponed so that you and your spouse can immediately focus on resolving the major issues in your divorce.

The first official step in the Collaborative process is almost always a four-way conference where you, your spouse, and both attorneys get together to discuss how you want the case to proceed.

During this initial conference, you, your spouse, and both attorneys will sign a Participation Agreement, which lays out a number of ground rules designed to provide a safe and effective environment for settlement. In signing the agreement, you're all promising to resolve all of your issues out of court and abide by the ground rules. To get a better idea of what's covered in a typical Participation Agreement, take a look at Appendix A.

Technically, however, all legal divorces, even Collaborative ones, do start with a petition. But, in Collaborative cases, rather than having one spouse serve a petition on the other party, where available a Joint Petition is prepared in which you and your spouse petition for the divorce together. This Joint Petition is signed by both you and your spouse. It does not have to be "served on" anyone.

Step Three: Taking Care of Immediate Problems

Even under the best of circumstances, it may take months—or sometimes even years, in high-conflict cases—to resolve each and every issue of the divorce. In the meantime, though, there are almost always a number of matters that need to be resolved immediately. These may include who will reside in the house, how much time the children will spend at each home, how certain bills initially will be paid, and whether one party pays temporary support to the other.

In divorce terminology, these immediate concerns are called *temporary issues*, so that there is a clear distinction between them and the *final* agreements you and your spouse eventually will reach.

As the name implies, agreements on temporary issues are tempo-rary, meaning that everyone understands that the resolution is *not final, and that* it may be renegotiated later.

The Traditional Method: Creating New Problems

In a traditional divorce process, you and your spouse would have very little direct communication with each other. As a result, one or both of you might become very anxious about issues that need to be dealt with immediately. If you and your spouse can't agree on how to handle these temporary issues, your attorney may urge you to seek an emergency court order at a temporary hearing.

During the hearing, you and your attorney submit a list of these issues to the judge by filing a motion (a request for help) and affi-davits (sworn statements). These affidavits, written by you and oth-ers on your behalf, lay out all of the reasons that you should get the things you are seeking, such as temporary custody, temporary pos-session of the house, or temporary child support. Your spouse's at-torney then submits similar papers explaining why your spouse should get what he or she wants, and *not* give you what you want.

After these papers have been filed with the court, you, your spouse, and your attorneys go to a courtroom where the attorneys make arguments to the judge that support each client's requests. Eventually the judge will issue a *temporary order* that addresses the temporary issues.

Disadvantages of the Traditional Method

As you can imagine, all those motions and affidavits and hearings are extremely expensive, but that's just the beginning. These tem-porary hearings are a classic example of a cure being worse than the disease.

Because the issues involved are so important to the couple (custody of the children, for example) these very public affidavits all too often contain hurtful and exaggerated statements that can't be taken back. Because these statements become a permanent part of the public record, they often create a great deal of animosity between spouses, sometimes leaving scars that can take years to heal.

Even with the best of intentions, it's nearly impossible for judges to resolve temporary issues in a way that satisfies both parties. The limited amount of information the court receives, the unreliability of the information, and the difficulty of regulating certain aspects of family life, often make it impossible for either party to get a decision that makes them feel like a winner. In many cases, *both* parties come out of these hearings with the feeling that they lost.

Finally, temporary hearings often resolve only a few issues at a time, which means it often takes more hearings to resolve all issues.

Once the temporary issues have been decided, you and your spouse will start addressing *permanent* solutions. But by that time you'll have used up a lot of your financial and emotional resources, and your ability to succeed at this most important task will have been diminished significantly. For most divorcing couples, starting off their journey with a first step in the wrong direction leaves them further from their goals than where they started—and they ever intended.

An Alternative: The Collaborative Method of Addressing Temporary Issues

In the Collaborative process, most temporary issues are handled at one of the initial four-way meetings. Because sometimes it can take months to get a court date, and weeks more for a judgment, resolving your short-term concerns out of court will save you and your spouse a lot of time and money. It also reduces the anger and hostility that courtroom battles can cause, allowing you to conserve your precious financial and emotional resources for long-term solutions.

Step Four: Gathering and Exchanging Information

In order for your case to be resolved, everyone—you, your spouse, your attorneys, and the court—has to have a clear understanding of all the facts that could possibly affect your case. These facts usually include information about the value of your assets (your house, your stock funds, and so on), your and your spouse's income, and the basic monthly expenses for your family (if you and your spouse are no longer living under one roof).

Obviously, to make sure everyone has the same information, you and your spouse are going to have to exchange a lot of documents. Some (pay stubs, mortgage coupons, cancelled checks, credit card statements, and so on) will be easy to locate. Others, such as the value of your house or retirement accounts, may take more effort to gather or obtain.

This exchange of information and gathering of facts can be handled informally (such as you and your spouse simply gathering the necessary papers and making copies for each other) or through more formal methods.

The Traditional Method: Formal Discovery, Interrogatories, and Depositions

Courts in all communities have rules that require you and your spouse to make information available to each other. In a traditional divorce, attorneys often collect and exchange that information through a formal process called *discovery*. Discovery includes *interrogatories* (questions written by your attorney that your spouse must answer, and vice versa), *requests for documents* (a demand to produce documents you may have), or *depositions* (having your spouse's attorney ask you questions under oath, or vice versa).

Disadvantages of the Traditional Method

As with so many of the other aspects of traditional divorce, gathering information through formal methods is often expensive, time consuming, and invasive. In most cases, it shouldn't be all that difficult for you and your spouse to find out what each of you has. But in the traditional divorce, you and your spouse wouldn't be communicating with each other directly. So your attorneys, worried that they might miss something, will play it safe by asking for anything and everything that could conceivably exist in your case. They'll often demand thousands of pages of documents or conduct lengthy depositions. While being overly inclusive may help lawyers sleep better at night (knowing that nothing has been overlooked), it creates an enormous expense for you that is not necessarily in your interest.

In addition, the burden of having to provide all of this information can be so great that it is often used as a strategic advantage. Your spouse, for example, may force you to spend many hours and thousands of dollars gathering information with the hope of using up your resources so you'll be more inclined to settle the case. More often than not, this strategy backfires, since you'd probably have your attorney level the playing field by making your spouse answer the same questions. Forcing each other to spend more on discovery, there are now fewer joint financial resources to divide, and that makes settlement a lot more difficult (and less lucrative for both of you).

Finally, the formal discovery process often generates too much of the wrong kind of information and very little of what you're really looking for. Yes, your spouse can be forced to provide documents and answer questions. But no discovery process can force him or her to give you candid answers about the things that matter most, such as their intentions regarding the children or their career, the real value of their business, and so on. The only way you or your spouse will be open and honest with each other is if you have a safe environment in which you can speak freely. Formal discovery tends to have the opposite effect, since both attorneys will advise their clients to reveal as little as possible, unless under duress.

An Alternative: The Collaborative Method of Gathering and Exchanging Information

In the Collaborative process, the Participation Agreement makes clear that you and your spouse must *voluntarily* disclose *all* relevant facts. Therefore, most Collaborative cases result in your having more information at a much lower cost, financially and emotionally.

Although the formalities are avoided, you'll still have the same opportunity to obtain all necessary information. At the same time, you and your spouse can control the process by deciding just how far you want to go with the information-gathering. As a practical matter, the two of you can choose to gather the information on your own or have the attorneys assist you in finding what they need. Because much information must be freely shared at the very beginning of the process, you won't have to spend countless hours digging up irrelevant documents or facts.

Perhaps most importantly, the Collaborative process focuses on creating a safe environment that allows you and your spouse to answer critical questions without worrying that the answers will be used against you. The Participation Agreement prohibits either party from using information provided in an adversarial manner. This allows both you and your spouse to have open and productive discussions about the important facts of your case.

Step 5: Using Experts

Because most divorce cases require you and your spouse to obtain information outside the expertise of your attorneys (the value of your home, business, pension, and so on), it's common to call in some experts to help resolve the issues.

The Traditional Method: Hiring the Experts

In a traditional divorce, each side hires its own expert to support its position. This is based on the assumption that you couldn't possibly trust an expert hired by your spouse. Naturally, he or she is thinking the same thing. It's then up to the court to decide which expert's opinion is closer to the truth.

Disadvantages of the Traditional Method of Retaining Experts

Having each side bring in its own hired guns to support its position often leads to unnecessary duplication and expense. And because your expert and your spouse's expert will inevitably contradict each other, the very facts you're trying to clarify end up more confused than ever. As a result, it's harder for the judge to determine which expert is more reliable, and how best to rule on the issue at hand.

An Alternative: The Use of Experts in the Collaborative Process

In the Collaborative process, only *neutral* experts are used. You and your spouse, with the help of your attorneys, agree on these neutral experts together. Most Collaborative attorneys have a list of outstanding experts in their area who have strong reputations for competence and impartiality. As you can imagine, this process saves time and money and allows everyone concerned to explore ways to find win-win solutions for both parties. For example, a neutral accountant might be able to help you and your spouse reduce the amount of taxes you'd owe after the divorce is final. Similarly, a neutral child psychologist might suggest parenting arrangements and ways of communicating that could help you and your spouse become better parents to your children.

Step Six: Negotiating a Settlement

At some point, you and your spouse, with the help of your attorneys, will turn to the issue of negotiating a settlement of all of the issues in your case. This process can be very informal (you and your spouse talking directly to each other) or very formal (you and your spouse and the attorneys negotiating at the courthouse under the direction of a judge).

The Traditional Method: Arguments and Conferences

In a traditional divorce, negotiations are generally handled by the attorneys and presented in the form of *arguments* (in the legal sense of the word) in favor of their client's positions. These arguments can come in many forms, including letters, *briefs* (formal statements made by the attorneys), conferences between the attorneys, conferences involving the attorneys and clients, and formal settlement conferences at the courthouse with a judge present. You and your spouse typically would not be directly involved in most aspects of the settlement discussions. Your desires and the arguments in favor of your position in general are conveyed through your attorney.

Disadvantages of the Traditional Method

You and your spouse have the best information about what your family needs. You—not your attorney—have the most at stake in the outcome of your case. Shutting you out of the negotiation process or forcing you to communicate indirectly generally reduces your chances of finding the best solutions. Formal methods of negotiation can be cumbersome and the arguments can often drive people further away from finding solutions. Also, attorneys tend to gravitate toward cookie-cutter solutions that work in many cases but may not address the unique needs of your family.

In addition, a lot of research has shown that the position-based method of negotiation is one of the *least productive* ways of reaching positive outcomes. Because both sides believe that the final resolution will come down to the judge splitting the difference, both sides tend to take more extreme positions, in an attempt to leave themselves more bargaining room. Unfortunately, this strategy results in both sides holding back their best offer until the end, sometimes in a high-drama, high-pressure negotiation on the courthouse steps. At that point, little room is left for creative problem-solving.

And while the attorneys are focused on making arguments and defending positions, some of the most critical interests of the clients—such as the welfare of the children—are neglected.

An Alternative: The Collaborative Method of Negotiating Solutions

Collaborative attorneys receive specialized training in interest-based conflict resolution. That means that their expertise is in helping you and your spouse identify big-picture goals and finding common ground so you can get better results. Unlike the traditional process in which the negotiations are handled primarily by the attorneys, the Collaborative process uses four-way meetings in which you and your spouse are present and active in the problem-solving. During these four-way meetings, your Collaborative attorney will be there to support you, but will rarely (if ever) resort to arguments and accusations.

Arguments by attorneys are rarely effective because they invariably cause the other spouse to become more entrenched in his or her positions and spend a lot of time coming up with counterarguments. Take a second and think of some of the arguments you've witnessed. How often did anyone change his or her mind midstream? Not often. You can see how ineffective the strategy of having lawyers argue on your behalf can be.

Collaborative attorneys are trained to avoid arguments and accusations in favor of more effective strategies, such as goal setting, active listening, identifying common interests, generating creative solutions, and maximizing outcomes. At each step in the process, your Collaborative attorney will help you understand and assess your options, leading you to make the best choices for you and your family.

Step Seven: Getting a Final Divorce Decree Through Stipulation or Trial

Your divorce will end in one of two ways: Either you and your spouse will reach an agreement or you will go to trial. In some cases, this "end" may actually be the beginning of an ongoing postdivorce battle, but the signing of the Final Decree by the judge formally dissolves the marriage and resolves, at least for the time being, all of the issues in the divorce.

The Traditional Method: Settlement, at a Cost—or Trial

As we mentioned earlier, more than 95 percent of all cases settle before going to trial. However, in the traditional process, that settlement may happen only after you and your spouse have been to court on one or more occasions, for temporary hearings, settlement conferences, and so on. Sometimes these cases settle within days or hours before the trial is scheduled to begin—after you and your spouse have already incurred most of the financial and emotional cost of preparing for trial.

If your case doesn't settle, it goes to trial. This means that you and your spouse may actually have to testify and provide other evidence, sometimes over the course of several days, with the hope that the judge will rule in your favor on most or all of the issues. At the end of the trial, the attorneys generally submit written arguments and proposals and the judge issues a decision, usually weeks or months after the trial. If either you or your spouse is unhappy with any part of the judge's decision, you can file an appeal with a higher court.

Disadvantages of the Traditional Process

Divorces that end by trial are usually very unsatisfying for both parties. The enormous financial and emotional expense and the inability of any judge to reach a final judgment that satisfies everyone makes it unlikely that you, your spouse, or your children will feel like winners in the end. As a result, the emotional scars from a divorce trial can last a lifetime.

Settlements that occur on the courthouse steps aren't much better. Last-minute decisions are made in the heat of the moment, after you've already paid out a lot of money and suffered through a great deal of acrimony leading up to trial.

An Alternative: The Collaborative Process of Finalizing the Divorce

In the Collaborative process, trials and hearings are eliminated and the final document is the result of an agreement signed by both you and your spouse. Besides addressing your immediate concerns, this agreement is designed to anticipate and avoid future problems. By engaging you and your spouse in the decision making, the Collaborative process often helps you both develop the skills to resolve future issues on your own, with minimal legal help. When the divorce is final, you and your spouse may still need to solve hundreds of problems on your own, going forward, particularly if you have children. If you learn how to do this during the divorce, you are more likely to be able to work these things out afterward in a mutually satisfying way.

Because agreements in the Collaborative process are not reached minutes before trial, there is a lot less pressure on you and your spouse and a lot more time spent identifying creative solutions that work best for you and your children. You'll also have plenty of time to secure any additional help you might need from other professionals, including mental health experts and financial specialists.

Step 8: Postdivorce Issues

While getting a divorce decree means that you're no longer married, many issues can linger. If you have minor children, for example, you and your spouse will need to find a way to cooperate with each other for many years to come. Even when there are no children, there still can be postdivorce issues, such as spousal support or agreements to pay property settlements over a period of years.

Postdivorce Issues in a Traditional Divorce

The acrimony that can occur in a traditional divorce can live for years in the form of posttrial motions, appeals, and attempts to change the court's decisions. If you believe that you "won" in court or received a more favorable settlement, your spouse may keep coming back in the hopes of correcting a perceived injustice.

Disadvantages of Traditional Methods

One of the biggest disadvantages of the traditional method is that it doesn't teach divorcing couples how to resolve conflicts on their own. So when even the smallest problems arise, they often feel that they have no option but to go to court. And that means more papers are filed, formal discovery is used to gather information, and more position-based negotiations take place, perhaps even new trials. The aforementioned disadvantages of the traditional method—in particular, the expense, duplication of effort, frustration, and anger—often get replayed, again and again, over the years, until both parties eventually are satisfied (unlikely) or run out of steam and money (more likely).

An Alternative: Postdivorce Issues in the Collaborative Process

Postdivorce issues in Collaborative cases are quite rare. There isn't anything to appeal because the final decision was decided by the couple, with individual legal counsel, and not forced on anyone. There is rarely a need to enforce the divorce decree since parties are always more apt to follow rules that they themselves have created. Even the issues that crop up in the future generally can be handled by applying the same principals that led to the agreement in the first place. Because the Collaborative process focuses on giving you and your spouse the tools to resolve your issues on your own, there's a very good chance that you'll be able to stay out of court.

Now that you've seen, step-by-step, how a Collaborative divorce differs from a traditional one, you can understand why there has been such an increase in the popularity of out-of-court strategies. Of course, Collaborative divorce is not the only way to resolve cases without going to trial. In chapter 2, we'll show you how Collaborative law compares to some of the common alternatives, including mediation.

CHAPTER 2

Divorce Alternatives:
Is the Collaborative Process Right for You?

In comparing our experience as traditional family lawyers to our experience as Collaborative lawyers, we believe that the Collaborative method offers the best way to end your marriage in the least expensive, least adversarial, and least hurtful way. Based on our work with hundreds of clients, we can also safely say that it's a way that will greatly improve your chances of getting what you want out of the divorce so you can move on with your life with confidence.

But as good as it is, Collaborative divorce is not the only alternative to the traditional divorce process. This chapter is devoted to helping you figure out whether Collaborative divorce truly is the best option for you. But before we do that, we'd like to introduce you to three other ways of reaching a settlement, and highlight how these methods differ from the Collaborative approach.

- Reaching an agreement on your own, with very little professional assistance
- Reaching a settlement with the help of a mediator
- Negotiating an agreement during the traditional litigation process (commonly referred to as a *litigated settlement*)

Reaching an Agreement on Your Own

This is the least formal and perhaps the most difficult option. With this approach, you and your spouse meet, without lawyers or other third parties present, at a restaurant or other public place for the purpose of working on your divorce settlement issues. (See Appendix B for a list of common marital issues.) Choosing a public venue is important because, after all, we're all on better behavior in front of others. You can use this approach to resolve as many issues as you choose, and it can also be an early step toward mediation or the Collaborative process.

To make this work, you and your spouse will need some basic knowledge of the legal effects of any agreements you might make. For that reason, each of you should have access to a lawyer (preferably a Collaborative lawyer) for advice and counseling outside of the conference with your spouse. You'll both need to have all your financial information, such as income statements, house and mortgage values, retirement and investment account balances, credit card statements, an so on fully available. Limit your sessions to one or two hours, with the understanding that either of you can leave if things get too intense. If you reach a tentative agreement, you'll need to put it in writing (plain, non-legalese English is fine).

Because you'll be working through these issues without any outside professional support, and because this process takes a high degree of emotional stability on your part and that of your spouse, it's successful for only about 10 percent of couples who attempt it. One caveat: This approach is absolutely *not* appropriate if there is an obvious power imbalance between you and your spouse (i.e., if, during the marriage, one of you made most of the decisions, overriding or ignoring the other's input).

How is this different from Collaborative law? With the Collaborative process, each party hires a supportive Collaborative lawyer who attends the meetings in order to best facilitate settlement.

Sam and Julie have been separated for six months, and after some fairly productive marriage counseling, have decided to divorce. They have no children. After consulting with Collaborative lawyers, who gave them lists of important topics to discuss, they decided to try to resolve their issues on their own. After gathering and sharing their financial information, they have been meeting for an agreed-upon hour and a half every two weeks at the local twenty-four-hour restaurant. Between meetings Sam and Julie have met with their attorneys to review progress and get clearer on the legal implications of the issues they are working to resolve. They both hope to have a rough outline of their agreement for submission to their attorneys following their next meeting.

Barbara and Lou, after consulting with their respective divorce lawyers, agreed to try the direct negotiation method to resolve their marital issues. Barbara is clear that she wants to divorce, but Lou has had difficulty adjusting to the idea. They met at a local restaurant for an initial session, during which Lou had a difficult time emotionally and kept making inappropriate, angry statements that Barbara found hurtful. Without the necessary support to make this process work, Barbara declined to continue, and each party is pursuing individual legal representation.

Mediation

Mediation first became available in the 1970s, as a way to avoid many of the pitfalls of traditional divorce proceedings. It attempts to work with the participants outside the court system, as do most other settlement options. Sessions include you, your spouse, and a mediator who is a trained neutral party who works with you and your partner to reach a settlement on all of your issues. The mediator may (or may not) be an attorney by training, but regardless is prohibited from giving you or your spouse any legal advice. This means that both you and your spouse should each have a lawyer outside the mediation process to advise you on legal issues.

The mediator meets with the two of you—usually without your attorneys—in sessions that generally last several hours. If you are successful in reaching an agreement, the mediator prepares a memorandum, which you submit to your respective attorneys for review, finalizing, and processing with the court. While some consider it an advantage to pay only one person for help in reaching an agreement, be aware that you may still need to retain two separate attorneys to draft and process the agreements reached in mediation.

As with direct negotiations between the parties, extreme power imbalances can be difficult for a mediator to counterbalance, sometimes making mediation a less viable option for couples for which this is a problem.

It is strongly recommended that parties attempting direct negotiations or mediation retain Collaborative lawyers to advise them, since mediators may be prohibited from offering this kind of advice, and these lawyers can provide clear legal counsel and have no agenda or motivation to escalate matters into litigation.

Litigated Settlements

Most traditional divorce lawyers will tell you that they settle almost all of their cases out of court. And the statistics would seem to back them up—in the vast majority of divorces that are headed for litigation, the divorcing couple arrives at a settlement without having the matter decided by a judge. However, there is a big difference between *litigated settlements* and settlements reached through out-of-court approaches.

Henry and Mary Lou attended an informational session with a Collaborative lawyer. In this session, the attorney mentioned, among other procedures, mediation. Henry and Mary decided to try it, and interviewed several mediators recommended by their lawyers. They chose to work with Susan, a practicing mediator with seven years' experience and a background in social work, as an alternative to Collaborative law.

Henry and Mary Lou filled out Susan's information sheets, providing all the financial and budgetary information, and started biweekly sessions at Susan's office. Susan's job was one of facilitation—attempting to draw out the agreements from the parties. Susan's presence and conflict-resolution skills enabled the parties to finesse much of the negativity typically present between divorcing couples, and Henry and Mary Lou took Susan's advice of having Collaborative lawyers on retainer to review and file the final agreement. Susan has kept the lawyers informed on the progress after each session, and, after four meetings, Susan believes the prognosis is good for final agreements after the next session.

Litigated settlements generally are made after much of the preparation for trial has been completed and most of the financial and psychological damage has already been done. They're also frequently made under pressure, forced by the party who seems to have the stronger case.

The Collaborative method incorporates the best elements of each of these options—and goes a step further. A natural fit between litigation and mediation, Collaborative law removes the court from the litigation model and offers the support and the legal expertise missing from the mediation model.* In addition to being a stand-alone

*Unless added as an adjunct by the parties.

> John and Judy, after much soul-searching and some marriage counsel-
> ing, have decided to divorce. In researching different divorce options,
> Judy heard about Collaborative law and visited the Web site of the In-
> ternational Academy of Collaborative Professionals (www.Collaborative
> practice.com). Judy was attracted to the description of the process and
> was referred to a local Collaborative attorney. She explained the results
> of her investigation to John, and they decided to explore the Collabo-
> rative option further.

settlement option, Collaborative law can serve as a supplement to the
mediation process and to assist parties seeking settlement on their
own.

As is likely obvious, we favor the Collaborative method over any
of the other available settlement options for the reasons previously
explained. However, we recognize that it's not appropriate for
everyone. The next section provides a quick test to help you determine whether a Collaborative divorce is right for you.

Finding Success with the Collaborative Process

It seems odd to talk about "success" with respect to divorce, particularly if you do not want the divorce to happen. But success with
the Collaborative process is best achieved when you are able to focus
on your most important goals. In order to determine whether the
Collaborative method is right for you, ask yourself the following:

- What matters most to you in life?
- What are the dreams you have for yourself and your family?
- What will stand out as most important when you look back
  at this part of your life twenty years from now?

Carol was still in so much pain after learning about Bob's new relationship that she found it nearly impossible to focus during their divorce. What Bob had done was wrong, and she wanted desperately for him and others to know how much he had hurt her.

Carol's attorney had advised her that the settlement that Bob was offering was more than a judge would order, and emphasized the benefits of not having to go to court. But to Carol, accepting Bob's offer felt like letting him off too easily.

Carol understood that her state had no-fault divorce laws and that she couldn't legally force Bob to agree to offer her more. But she felt that if Bob wanted this divorce, he was going to have to pay. So she rejected Bob's offer and held firm in her positions. Eventually, after two more very difficult months, Bob came around and offered her a settlement that was worth almost $20,000 more than his earlier offer. At last, Carol felt she had "won."

During the years that followed the divorce, Carol's bitter feelings toward Bob didn't heal. Getting a better settlement never gave her the sense of vindication that she had been seeking. Moreover, the goodwill or guilt that Bob seemed to show early in the divorce process eventually faded and, as a result, he responded to Carol's anger with his own bitterness. Their anger often spilled over to their parenting decisions, and because they still shared custody of their children, Carol and Bob found themselves fighting over issues concerning them at nearly every opportunity.

Looking back, more than fifteen years later, Carol can barely remember the details of the property settlement that seemed so important to her at the time. What she still remembers, all too well, is how painful it has all been, and not just for her, but for their kids.

Next week, Carol and Bob's oldest daughter, Anne, is getting married. For Carol, this should be one of the happiest moments of her life. Yet every thought of the wedding is accompanied by a lump in her throat when she imagines standing next to Bob and his new wife. She knows now that if she had it to do over again, she would have approached the divorce differently. She would have worked to achieve a resolution that would have left them both less bitter.

A "successful divorce" is one that puts you in the best position to achieve the broad goals that you've defined for yourself and, possibly, your children. Those goals might be quite different from the more immediate concerns that you're preoccupied with now. Focusing on the immediate need to "win" can cause you to lose focus on the things that, in the end, may be far more important, as you will see from the following scenario:

Is a Collaborative Divorce Right for You?

Based on our collective experience, we believe that a Collaborative divorce is by far the best and most successful option for most couples. But you are the best judge of your own goals and situation. Following is a short quiz that will help you determine whether the Collaborative method is your best option. After taking the test, we'll talk about some of the challenges you may face and help you determine whether they can be overcome.

Although you certainly can write in this book, we suggest that you make several copies of the pages that follow. Keep one for yourself and give the other to your spouse. For each statement below, circle the appropriate answer indicating how little or how much you agree. You'll learn what each of your answers means later.

	Strongly Disagree	Disagree	Neutral (or doesn't apply)	Agree	Strongly Agree
My ability to achieve a successful outcome in the divorce primarily will depend on the decisions I make during the process	1	2	3	4	5
In order to achieve my most important goals, I am willing to let go of some smaller, short-term issues, even though it may be very hard to do so	1	2	3	4	5
I am capable of making the emotional commitment necessary to achieve the best possible outcome	1	2	3	4	5
I am not afraid of or intimidated by my spouse	1	2	3	4	5

	Strongly Disagree	Disagree	Neutral (or doesn't apply)	Agree	Strongly Agree
I am willing to try to see things from my spouse's point of view in order to help achieve the best possible outcome	1	2	3	4	5
I believe it is possible for my spouse and me to restore enough trust in each other to achieve a successful outcome	1	2	3	4	5
I am willing to commit myself fully to resolving the issues through the Collaborative process by working toward common interests rather than simply arguing in favor of my positions	1	2	3	4	5

	Strongly Disagree	Disagree	Neutral (or doesn't apply)	Agree	Strongly Agree
It is important to me that my spouse and I maintain a respectful and effective relationship after the divorce	1	2	3	4	5
I have accepted the fact that this divorce is going to happen	1	2	3	4	5
I believe that it is very important that our children maintain a strong, healthy relationship with both parents	1	2	3	4	5

Interpreting Your Test Results

Once you've written down your answers, add up your score. If your total is higher than 40, there's a very good chance that the Collaborative process is a good fit for you. Assuming your spouse is also a good candidate (he or she should take the quiz separately), your chances for a successful outcome are very high. Reading the remainder of this chapter will help you identify and reinforce your strengths and shore up your weaknesses (any area in which you scored a 1 or 2 is a potential challenge and is worth examining).

If your total is between 30 and 40, you're still a good candidate for the Collaborative process. Be sure to read the rest of this chapter, focusing especially on your 1s and 2s.

If your total is between 20 and 30, you're borderline. The Collaborative process may work for you, but you'll have to do a lot of prep work to get there. Carefully study the challenges identified by your 1 and 2 answers, and consider what you need to do to become better prepared. You also might want to consider postponing the divorce, if possible, until you're ready to work toward the best possible outcome.

If your total is below 20, it's very likely that you'll become frustrated with the Collaborative process. And there's a good chance you'll find the alternatives equally frustrating. While it's still possible to succeed in the Collaborative process by resolving your case out of court, unless you make some significant changes in your perspective, you won't come through the Collaborative process feeling as if you've achieved your most important goals.

Putting Your Test Results in Perspective

Of course this test is simply a tool used to help identify challenges inherent in the Collaborative process, and help you to determine whether you are willing to meet them. Certainly, there are some circumstances, such as abuse or addiction, that may make collaboration impossible, regardless of how you scored on other aspects of the test. Regardless of your individual results, we urge you to read the rest of this chapter, paying particular attention to the areas where you indicated disagreement. Each statement is explored on its own.

Taking Personal Responsibility.

"My ability to achieve a successful outcome in the divorce primarily will depend on the decisions I make as I go through the process."

One of the most important indicators of success in the Collaborative process is your ability to take personal responsibility for your role in resolving the issues at hand. If you disagree with this statement and want to consider the Collaborative method, you'll need to rethink this position. It doesn't matter whether the divorce was your idea or not, or who (if anyone) was most responsible for the breakup of the marriage. In the Collaborative process, you and your spouse have much more control over how your case turns out than any judge, attorney, or evaluator. But with control comes responsibility. So you must decide if you are willing to accept the responsibility and to do the hard work necessary to achieve success through this process.

And no, you're not the only one who needs to take responsibility. Your spouse will, as will the professionals you hire (including the attorneys). But since the ultimate responsibility for the outcome lies with you and your spouse, your success will depend on your ability to accept your share of that responsibility.

Playing the Blame Game

One of the advantages of the traditional process is that if things go wrong (and they often do), there's always someone around to blame: your spouse, his or her attorney, the judge, your attorney, the system, choose one! Holding someone else accountable for your situation may give you a temporary sense of relief during a difficult time, but if you opt to pursue a divorce through the Collaborative method, you'll need to trade in that warm blanket of blame for the cold reality of personal responsibility. If you're willing to pay that price, the results can be well worth it.

Role of the Attorneys

One thing that can stand in the way of your success with the Collaborative method is the belief that your attorney is responsible for solving your problems. In the traditional adversarial method, it's common to harbor the fantasy that your attorney will make the perfect argument, leading to your ultimate vindication. While you may understand that your attorney won't be making courtroom arguments, in a Collaborative case, you may still cling to the belief that your attorney will find "the" solution.

Whether you're considering the Collaborative process or a traditional model, it's important to grasp early on that attorneys do *not* solve your problems—imagining they do will cause only disappointment. At best, Collaborative attorneys are responsible for guiding you through the process in a way that maximizes your chance to achieve the best possible results. While an effective attorney can be very valuable in helping you help yourself, the ultimate responsibility for the outcome of your case remains with you and your spouse.

Seeing the Big Picture

"In order to achieve my most important goals, I am willing to let go of some smaller, short-term issues, even though it may be very hard to do so."

People who achieve the greatest success in the Collaborative process are those who are best able to take a few steps back and remind themselves of what is truly important. For some people, the urgency of smaller problems can be so overwhelming that it becomes nearly impossible to take a broader view of things.

In the heat of a divorce proceeding, it's easy to let your mind gravitate toward immediate concerns, issues that need to be resolved in order to stabilize your situation and create a safe environment for settlement. But from time to time in the Collaborative process, you'll be asked to divert your attention from the immediate concerns and focus on more permanent long-term goals. For example, you may need to ask yourselves questions such as "How will this decision affect my ability to co-parent in the long run?" And you need to be clearheaded enough to answer.

The big-picture issues generally are the ones that will matter more to you in the future than now. When you imagine yourself looking back on your divorce twenty years from now, what do you think will matter the most? Will it have been the custody "label" that you used, or how the children fared? Will it be the exact dollar amounts of your property division, or the fact that you emerged from the divorce with your self-respect intact? If you find it hard to ask and answer these questions because you're more focused on immediate issues, you may find yourself becoming frustrated with the long-range view required by the Collaborative process.

One of the advantages of having practiced law for several decades is that we've both had the opportunity to reconnect with clients we represented ten, even twenty years ago. Even clients who "won" in court often wound up upset with the damage that litigation did to their lives over the long haul. On the flip side, those who made seemingly painful compromises in the short term in favor of meeting their big-picture goals seemed, unanimously, to have reaped the rewards.

Many of Joyce's friends told her she was being foolish for not going to court to demand that Mike pay more child support.

Yes, she could have asked for full custody and the child support to go with it, but there was a lot to the story that her friends couldn't fully understand. Joyce felt that allowing Mike to spend more time with their children would work out best in the long run, even if that meant a lower child-support payment. In addition, Mike had made some other concessions that she felt, over time, would turn out to be more important to her. For example, Mike had agreed to participate in family counseling to help their son Joey adjust to the divorce. He had also been willing to make sure the children attended her church on his weekends, even though he did not share her religious beliefs. Still, when Joyce tried to explain this to her friends, they accused her of giving in too easily.

To Joyce, it just didn't make sense to try to push Mike to the financial limit of the law, even if she could. After all they'd been through, Joyce admitted that she didn't like Mike very much as a person. But despite his faults, Joyce was able to remind herself that Mike was still a great father who had a close relationship with all three of their children.

Twelve years later, when Joyce looks back on her divorce, she can't remember the financial details—and she has no real recollection of who got the better deal. She does remember, though, that somehow she and Mike managed to make it all work out: the changes in the parenting schedule, the adjustment in support when Mike lost his job, the extension of her spousal support when she was unable to finish her education on schedule. None of it was easy, and there were times that she and Mike disagreed over serious matters. But they came out with their dignity intact and their family as close to whole as was possible in their situation. More importantly, their children didn't get caught in the middle.

Joyce and Mike both are excited about the arrival of their first grandchild in May. Joyce still feels some sadness when she thinks of the circumstances of her divorce, but she doesn't spend much time thinking about it anymore. She is happy in her new life, proud of the fact that she was able to get through this dark period with her head held high and move on.

Emotions

"I am capable of making the emotional commitment necessary to achieve the best possible outcome."

Divorce is complicated by the fact that it generally involves far more than legal issues. In many cases, the emotional component of a divorce may be as critical, or even more critical, than who gets what. But because our legal system doesn't offer an adequate framework for addressing issues of the heart, it tends to emphasize only the items or expenses that can be listed on a balance sheet. But the disappointment, sadness, and betrayal of divorce often don't just disappear on their own. Left unattended, these feelings can magnify to the point where they pose serious impediments to reaching a settlement or maintaining a durable (manageable) agreement in the years after the divorce.

We all know that strong emotions can hinder our ability to make clear, rational decisions, and it is likely that your impending divorce is one of the most difficult emotional challenges you and/or your spouse have ever faced. And yet one of the unfortunate realities of divorce is that people are often asked to make some of the most important decisions of their lives at a time when they are the least equipped to do so.

Since success with the Collaborative process depends on the quality of the decisions you make, you have the option of addressing your emotions through a variety of ways, including hiring a divorce coach or delaying the divorce until you have had time to make the emotional adjustment. You are also given the freedom to address the emotional aspects of the divorce at any stage in the process. However, if you are someone who is uncomfortable using such tools, your opportunities for success with the Collaborative method may be limited.

Your General Emotional Health

The emotional impact of divorce, when combined with such common mental-health issues as depression, sometimes can render you unable to participate in the decision-making process effectively. If you believe that your emotional health has deteriorated to the point where your ability to make sound decisions is seriously compromised, you may need to consider the possibility of postponing the divorce, or at least some aspects of it, until you're emotionally stronger. While your spouse may be reluctant to want to allow things to drag on indefinitely, it may be possible to negotiate a delay by finding out what your spouse needs in order to make a delay a possible alternative.

Addiction or Codependency Issues

In considering the Collaborative process, it's important for you to honestly assess whether you suffer from any addictions, such as alcoholism, drug addiction, or compulsive gambling. It's also essential to consider whether you have codependency issues as a result of living with someone who is addicted. Either of these conditions can severely affect your ability to make important decisions. And your success with the Collaborative process ultimately will depend on your willingness to get the help you need. One of the goals of the Collaborative process is to create a safe environment in which you can seek assistance without the fear that acknowledging the problem will weaken your position or put you at a disadvantage in the settlement negotiations.

Fear and Intimidation

"I am not afraid of or intimidated by my spouse."

Feeling afraid of or intimidated by your spouse raises some special concerns for Collaboration, such as:

- Is there a marked imbalance of power between the parties?
- Is there a climate of distrust?
- Do the parties engage in blaming and name-calling?
- Does one or the other of the parties want to control everything?

The Collaborative process can work effectively only in a safe environment, so it's important for your lawyers to know as much as possible about how these patterns existed in your marriage. They can then assist you in coming up with procedures to counteract these tendencies when working Collaboratively.

Intimidation and Other Power Imbalance Issues

Even without a history of abuse, you may still feel intimidated by your spouse as a result of other dynamics in your relationship. And even if there isn't direct intimidation, there may be a power imbalance in your relationship. In many marriages, one spouse "wears the pants," playing a more dominant role. That additional power may be the result of a variety of factors, ranging from the degree of financial sophistication that each person possesses to the manner in which you each handle anger and fear. Depending on your particular situation, you will need to consider the impact that this will have on your divorce negotiations.

What If There Has Been a History of Domestic Abuse?

Some experts maintain that victims of domestic abuse should never use Collaborative law, mediation, or any method of dispute resolution that is not centered around a court of law. We disagree. In many cases, the Collaborative process can be a very effective alternative—as long as you and your spouse commit to the Collaborative process and acknowledge the past history of violence.

If there has been any domestic abuse in your relationship, you must be completely honest with your attorneys, and you'll need to consider whether the dynamics between you and your spouse will affect your ability to negotiate an agreement. You may also need to consult with a mental-health professional who has worked with abusers and survivors in order to accurately assess your situation.

If you have been the victim of abuse, you'll want to make sure that you're not put in an unsafe environment where you may feel physically or emotionally threatened. If you are truly afraid of physical harm from your spouse, the Collaborative process can't work; you may need to seek legal protection and more traditional proceedings.

If you have abused your spouse, the Collaborative process can work *only* if you understand your behavior and are sincerely willing to agree to *whatever* action is necessary to allow your spouse to feel safe.

The Less Powerful Spouse

Being the less powerful spouse when it comes to conflict resolution doesn't mean that you'll be at a disadvantage with the Collaborative approach. In fact, handled skillfully, it can better address power imbalances than any other method, setting a positive precedent for future interactions. The key is finding and working with professionals who support you and help to create an environment where you feel completely comfortable expressing your ideas and interests.

The More Powerful Spouse

If you see yourself as the more powerful spouse emotionally, financially, or psychologically, if you feel that you need to control the direction of every discussion, or if you have a tendency to anger easily or use intimidation to get what you want, you'll need to change your behavior for the Collaborative process to work. While these strategies may, on occasion, make you feel that you've won the battle, the residual negativity will likely have a more detrimental effect on your long-term goals than you realize. Skilled Collaborative practitioners (attorneys, coaches, so on) will work to prevent anyone from trying to intimidate or exercise an undue amount of control over the process. If you believe their intervention will be difficult for you, you'll need to consider whether the Collaborative process is truly a good fit for your particular personality.

Seeing and Understanding Your Spouse's Point of View

"I am willing to try to see things from my spouse's point of view in order to help achieve the best possible outcome."

A strong indicator of success in the Collaborative process is your ability to empathize with your spouse. By that we mean the ability to listen to your spouse and understand his or her perspective. You don't have to agree with what's being said—but you do need to understand it. If you're unable or unwilling to put yourself in your spouse's shoes, you'll likely have trouble benefiting from the Collaborative process.

It's not easy to listen when you're angry with your spouse. You may be thinking, "Why should I empathize with his needs, after what he did to me?" The short answer is that it's in *your own* best interest. While showing empathy may indeed *seem* like the nice thing to do, as Collaborative attorneys we're less concerned about being nice than being *smart*. The more carefully you listen to what your spouse is saying is important to him or her, the more readily you will find the keys to a solution that you will both find acceptable.

If you believe that you might have some trouble empathizing, you may be able to improve in this area by using coaches (see chapter 4) or by selecting an attorney who is particularly strong in this area (see chapter 3).

Building Trust

"I believe it is possible for my spouse and me to restore enough trust in each other to achieve a successful outcome."

For some people, asking spouses in the middle of a divorce to trust each other may seem like a contradiction in terms. ("How can I trust someone who cheated on me?" or "If we trusted each other, we wouldn't be getting a divorce!")

There's a common misperception that trust is a black-and-white issue—either it's completely present or completely absent in a relationship. The truth is, in most situations only a *degree* of trust exists.

For example, allowing yourself to be in the same room with someone generally means that you trust that he or she isn't going to harm you. If you allow your children to be in the care of someone, even for a short time, you are demonstrating some level of trust that this person will not harm your children. Things will happen over the course of a relationship to increase or decrease this level of trust. Overall, trust is generally something that's earned through repeat behavior.

In a marriage, trust increases and decreases as each individual keeps or breaks promises, small or large. If you were to chart your trust levels over the course of your marriage, you'd likely discover that it's gone up and it's gone down, sometimes pretty dramatically. You'd probably also find that, now, in the face of divorce, it's at an all-time low.

While it may be hard to predict, it's important to try to antici-pate what level of trust you'll have in your spouse, in this process, even in yourself, from here on out. Believe it or not, it's actually pos-sible for trust between a couple to *increase* during the divorce pro-cess. Similarly, it's possible for trust to be significantly damaged during the divorce process, sometimes beyond repair ("I don't even know her!" and "That's not the man I married!" are common re-frains). That's why "winning," in the traditional context of divorce, is an illusion. If one of you wins in court and irreparably damages the trust in your relationship, have you really accomplished what you set out to do?

One of the most valid reasons for choosing the Collaborative process may be its potential for enhancing some measure of trust or, at a minimum, avoiding further damage to the relationship. How-ever, in order to make it work, you must be willing to attempt to trust, even in small measurable things, and you must be willing to engage in trustworthy behavior in order to restore some integrity to the relationship.

Committing to the Process

"I am willing to commit myself fully to resolving the issues through the Collaborative process by working toward com-mon interests rather than simply arguing in favor of my posi-tions."

Success in the Collaborative process is directly related to your commitment to making the process work. If you're considering Collaborative divorce because you think it'll be cheaper and faster, and you have no real commitment to making it work, you'll be disappointed. But if you're prepared to work hard on things such as listening, brainstorming creative solutions to seemingly irresolvable situations, and honestly evaluating your weaknesses, and you're willing to commit the necessary time and resources, you'll have a much better chance at a positive outcome.

Time

You are more likely to have a successful Collaborative divorce if you're willing to be patient and plan carefully.

There is a natural urge for most people to rush the process by focusing only on short-term goals and moving immediately to the negotiation of tough issues. While sticking points are inevitable in most negotiations, if you have thoroughly prepared prior to reaching that point, you will be more confident (and less panicked) that you will reach an acceptable solution.

Resources

Fully committing to the Collaborative process may also involve a willingness to commit the resources necessary to successfully resolve your issues. Even though the Collaborative method is almost always much cheaper than litigation, for people who are focused only on cost it will never seem cheap enough.

The desire to preserve your financial resources is certainly understandable. The financial demands of divorce draw on economic resources when they are least available. However, focusing on the cheapest solution may cause you to miss out on the most important benefits of a Collaborative divorce. Collaborative law is more about the quality of the settlement than about speed and cost.

The Postdivorce Relationship

"It is important to me that my spouse and I maintain a respectful and effective relationship after the divorce."

You are more likely to have success with the Collaborative process if you recognize that it's to your benefit to have at least a civil relationship with your spouse after the divorce. It's easiest to understand when children are involved, but it can be true in other cases as well.

If You Have Young Children

If you have young children, it should be fairly obvious why the quality of the postdivorce relationship with your spouse is important. But we've seen divorcing clients who, out of anger or sadness, come into our offices saying, "I never want to have to deal with this person again." While that's a very understandable emotion, your children's well-being may depend on your ability to build a functional postdivorce relationship. If you don't see value in working toward that goal, you may not be a good candidate for a Collaborative divorce.

If You Have Grown Children

Even if your children are grown, it is likely that you have a stake in the quality of your relationship with them and, by association, with the other parent. Many prior clients report that one of the things they value most about their Collaborative divorce is their ability to work with the other parent on issues affecting their adult children. Being able to feel comfortable attending college graduations, weddings, and births of grandchildren when their ex-spouse is present is very important to these clients and their children.

If You Have No Children

Many divorcing couples express a strong desire to either maintain a friendship with their ex-spouse, stay in contact with in-laws and mutual friends, or preserve the memory of the relationship. Resolving the divorce with dignity and respect will help you achieve these goals.

Acceptance

"I have accepted the fact that this divorce is going to happen."

Much of the success of the Collaborative process depends on accepting the divorce. But what if one of you doesn't want it to happen at all? It's hard to focus on divorce-related goals when your main hope is to reconcile the marriage. If you and your spouse share an interest in reconciling, by all means focus every effort on that goal! But if only one of you believes reconciliation is possible, the issue becomes much more complicated.

Psychological Divorce and Legal Divorce

The phrase *psychological divorce* is used to describe the actual emotional acceptance of the fact that a marriage is over. Psychological divorce often occurs on a completely different timeline than legal divorce—sometimes earlier, often later. In addition, while you and your spouse are required to proceed through the legal divorce

Saving the Marriage: What to Do When Reconciliation Is Possible

If your spouse has clearly stated that he or she is not willing to work on the marriage, your only choice may be to work on accepting that decision. However, if both of you are at least willing to explore the possibility of saving the marriage, you need to fully explore your options.

Your Collaborative lawyer probably won't have the professional background to counsel you about the particular methods that you should choose in working on your marriage. However, he or she may be able to recommend counselors, religious organizations, support groups, retreats, books, or other resources that you can investigate on your own.

If You're Uncertain About Your Spouse's Willingness to Work on the Marriage

If you are uncertain as to whether your spouse is willing to work on reconciliation, try to find a way to have a frank discussion about the issue. If you can't, raise your concern with your attorney and ask him or her to help you address it with your spouse. Your attorney may suggest a variety of options, including meeting with counselors or coaches to help create the right environment. It may also be possible to address this issue during a four-way meeting, although this is unlikely because of the absence of mental-health professionals with expertise in reconciliation issues.

Concerns About the Delays Caused by Reconciliation Efforts

If either you or your spouse is reluctant to work on the marriage because you're worried that the delay may have an adverse impact on the outcome of your divorce, discuss this with your attorneys. Your Collaborative attorneys probably can help you reach temporary agreements to address these concerns so that neither you nor your spouse will be penalized for taking time to work on reconciliation.

> *Collaborative Cases Can End in Reconciliation*
>
> No divorce process can save marriages—that decision needs to come from the couple. However, when a safe and effective environment for problem solving can be maintained, the range of outcomes can be very wide and, on occasion, even reconciliation can reappear as an option.

at the same pace, it is possible you will proceed through the emotional divorce at a very different pace. In some instances, both spouses may have experienced the psychological divorce long before one or the other chose to take legal action. Although the delay in attending to the legal divorce sometimes can take its toll, these couples have some advantage when the legal divorce has started because they both feel emotionally ready to move ahead.

You're Ready, He's Not

In a perfect world, the legal divorce could wait until both spouses had caught up emotionally. In the real world, however, the person who has emotionally accepted the divorce often feels a need to move ahead, even if the other spouse has not reached a point of emotional acceptance.

When one spouse is ready to end the marriage and the other is not, divorce lawyers often refer to the issue as "leaver/leavee." These situations present unique considerations that need to be addressed in the Collaborative process. In almost all jurisdictions today, it takes only one person to proceed with a divorce. Therefore, the divorce is almost certain to happen, even if one person believes the marriage can be saved. However, in the Collaborative process, it's important to acknowledge when one person doesn't want the divorce and to prepare to deal with the emotional issues that may arise as a result.

He's Ready, You're Not

If you didn't initiate the divorce, you may be feeling a great deal of sadness, anger, loss, and fear. You may also believe that your spouse should be held accountable for what he or she has done to you, or for forsaking your wedding vows. These feelings may run the gamut, from simply wanting some acknowledgment of the wrongdoing to wanting a more favorable settlement.

It's important, though, to come to grips with the fact that there's nothing you can do legally to stop your spouse from moving ahead with a divorce if he or she really wants it. If you're not emotionally ready, you may have difficulty making critical decisions necessary to start your new life, which makes it understandable that you might want to slow down the process.

There may, in fact, be ways to put things off for a while, but there also may be significant negative consequences to delaying the divorce. Your spouse may resent your efforts to unilaterally delay the divorce, causing much of the goodwill to erode and making settlement much more difficult when the hard issues have to be addressed. In addition, delaying some decisions, such as the decision to separate, may create tension in your home that could have an adverse emotional impact on your children. You should carefully consider these consequences before voicing your desire to delay.

In the Collaborative process, you may be able to negotiate a delay in order to make the emotional adjustment. To get your spouse to agree, you'll likely have to help him or her see that you are taking steps to move toward the adjustment. You may also need to reach certain temporary agreements to assure him or her that the delay will not work to his or her strategic disadvantage. The hope is that your spouse can see that the delay will also serve his or her interests since you both will be more ready to resolve issues once you fully engage in the process.

In the midst of the divorce process, some couples decide to attend marriage closure counseling in which they, with a mental-health professional, try to get to an emotionally similar place, to help them grieve the loss of marriage, or deal with unresolved issues. Others choose to work with divorce coaches. Still others negotiate a pace for the divorce that will help the "slower" spouse better make the adjustment.

When Delay Is Not Possible

If you're unable to agree to delay the divorce, or if the delay ends before you have reached a point of emotional acceptance, you may have no choice but to move ahead. As you might guess, this presents a unique set of problems. The fact that you aren't ready may cause you to resist reaching an agreement, either out of anger or resentment, or because you are finding yourself emotionally incapable of making decisions. This makes collaboration difficult, since, even if you don't intend it, it may appear that you and your spouse are working toward cross-purposes.

The Collaborative process does offer additional options that may help you and your spouse resolve the issue of being in different places. For example, you and your spouse could work with divorce coaches to help each of you communicate your needs more effectively and help you gain a better understanding of what each of you is saying. In addition, there are divorce-closure counselors who can help you and your spouse address underlying frustrations that may be getting in the way of your ability to resolve some of the key divorce issues. The role that coaches and counselors may play in your case is further discussed in chapter 4.

Realities and Challenges

Acknowledging the Realities of Your Situation

While the issue of who initiated the divorce may not be legally relevant, it will very likely affect the divorce process. In most cases, it is best to acknowledge this so that you can reach sound decisions about the pace of the process and best address this dynamic. Sometimes acknowledging the issue can lead to apologies or therapeutic intervention to help with the healing and emotional adjustment.

While acknowledgment of the circumstances of the divorce may be possible, punishing the "wrongdoer" is another matter. If you have a strong desire to punish your spouse for what he or she has done, you will need to work with your attorney and hopefully your coach and/or therapist to find better ways of addressing your emotional needs.

When You're the Leavee

The Collaborative process, as discussed, is generally far less painful than litigation. While this is almost always regarded as a positive thing, sometimes the "leavee" feels or fears this is letting the other spouse "off too easily." This may tempt the leavee to lean toward a litigation system either out of spite, or to make it harder for the leaving spouse to get out of the marriage.

It is true that the litigation process, because it can be extremely expensive and uncomfortable, can be used to inflict a certain amount of pain on the other person. However, generally it cannot be done without inflicting an equal or greater amount of pain on you and your children.

Your greatest challenge may be to separate your emotional needs from the critical legal decisions that you will need to make. If there are legitimate things that your spouse may be able to do to help you make the adjustment (such as coaching, divorce-closure counseling, slowing the process down, and so on) you can work with your attorney or coach to request your spouse's participation.

If You're the Leaver

Look honestly at the full impact of your decision. While you can't be held legally accountable for your decision to leave, the Collaborative model gives you the opportunity to consider whether it is in your best interests to attempt to repair some of the damage in the relationship through acknowledgment, affirmation, or even apologies, if appropriate. In addition, you may need to be patient in allowing your spouse to process the psychological divorce before the legal divorce can be complete.

If you are the leaver, and have already been through the psychological divorce, you may be eager for the legal divorce to be completed as well. However, your desire to move through the divorce quickly can raise significant problems, as your spouse is not likely to be ready to end the marriage as quickly and may resent your desire to "put this all behind you" as soon as possible. Similarly, if you believe your spouse is intentionally slowing the process down, you may become (understandably) frustrated by the delays.

Children Need Effective Relationships with Both Parents

"I believe that it is very important that our children maintain a strong, healthy relationship with both parents."

In situations involving children, the Collaborative process works best when the adults involved recognize that children need to have full, healthy relationships with both parents. That doesn't mean that the parenting has to be exactly equal. Rather, it means that there must be a shared goal of preserving and enhancing both parental relationships.

If you're in a situation in which you don't believe your children will benefit from a loving relationship with your spouse, you may have considerable difficulty with the Collaborative pro-

Ed and Karen chose to use the Collaborative process because they wanted to protect their children, Emily, age twelve, and Joe, age nine, from unnecessary acrimony. Karen had been home with the children during much of their preschool years, and she and Ed agreed that Karen's home should be the children's primary residence. However, Ed had always been a very involved father and didn't want to become a "visitation dad." Karen wanted to allow the children to spend a great deal of time at Ed's home but was concerned about Ed's alcohol abuse. Ed acknowledged that his drinking had increased during the past few years, but he claimed that it was primarily the result of trying to escape the mounting tension in their marriage.

In reality, Ed knew he had a problem but feared that if he admitted it, he would automatically be labeled an alcoholic and his time with the children would be limited or supervised. After two four-way meetings and some work with his divorce coach, Ed came to realize that, unlike in a traditional divorce setting, his candor about his drinking would not be used against him, and that he'd actually be more likely to get a liberal visitation schedule if Karen knew he was actively addressing the problem.

Ed enrolled in an alcohol dependency program recommended by a counselor. As Karen saw that Ed was addressing the problem, she became increasingly comfortable expanding Ed's visitation rights. Eventually they reached an agreement that allowed Ed to have a full schedule with the children, provided he continued to follow the counselor's recommendations regarding his alcohol use.

cess. We recognize that there are some parents who, because of mental illness, addiction, patterns of abuse, or other problems, aren't capable of maintaining healthy relationships with their children without undergoing radical change. If those parents are working toward recovery there is still a good chance that the Collaborative method can facilitate that. On the other hand, if a parent is unable or unwilling to create a safe environment in which to parent his or her children, it's extremely unlikely that the Collaborative process—or any other out-of-court settlement option—will work.

We trust this chapter has provided adequate information as to whether the Collaborative process is right for you. In the next part of this book, you'll take the first steps in the Collaborative process—getting your spouse to agree to the Collaborative approach and assembling a team of experts, starting with your Collaborative attorney.

PART TWO

Getting Others on Board

Putting Together Your Team

Now that you are ready to move ahead with the Collaborative process, it's time to get the other members of your team in place—starting with your spouse, followed by your attorney and your spouse's attorney. There are also a host of other professionals whose help you might need or at least find useful, such as divorce coaches, child specialists, and financial specialists. You'll note that we've placed the section on talking to your spouse about the Collaborative process before the section on hiring attorneys. Depending on your circumstances, you may want to reverse this. Here are a few guidelines that may help you determine whether your next step should be talking to your spouse or finding a lawyer:

When to Talk to Your Spouse Before Hiring an Attorney

- **When you're convinced that your spouse will embrace the idea of a Collaborative divorce** (either based on things he or she has said, or based on your general knowledge of your spouse), that's the place to start. This reinforces the idea that you're doing this as a couple instead of having the idea forced on one of you. It allows you and your spouse to coordinate your search and will greatly improve your chances for achieving a successful Collaborative outcome.

• **When you believe your spouse will have a negative reaction to your having hired an attorney first.** Finding out that you have been searching for an attorney may make your spouse suspicious and wary, even if your goal is not to create an unfair advantage. Fear and suspicion are common when couples are nearing a divorce decision, and it doesn't take much for those feelings to escalate into panic, anger, or retaliation.

If you believe that your spouse won't take the news well, it's probably best to first initiate a discussion about Collaborative divorce and then let him or her know that you're looking for an attorney who can help you both better understand the process. Being honest and forthright will go a long way toward reassuring your spouse that your motives are honest and for the betterment of both of you.

When to Hire an Attorney Before Talking to Your Spouse

• **When you feel uncertain.** If you feel unsure about how to present the idea of Collaborative divorce to your spouse, or if you still have questions about the process in general, you might be better off finding an attorney first. Besides being able to answer your questions, an attorney will be able to give you some ideas about the best ways to approach your spouse, given your particular circumstances. He or she may also have brochures or other written materials that can facilitate a productive discussion with your spouse.

- **When you have concerns about your spouse's initial reaction to the divorce.** Among other things, your attorney can suggest a number of ways to introduce the idea (such as in a therapeutic setting), which your spouse is less likely to perceive as hostile.

CHAPTER 3

Getting Your Spouse to Agree to the Collaborative Process, and How to Hire an Attorney

How to Talk to Your Spouse

You've compared the basic steps of the traditional divorce against Collaborative divorce. You've reviewed the alternatives, such as mediation, and you've decided to opt for a Collaborative divorce. Good choice! But you should also know by now that you can't do it alone.

So what's the best way to get your spouse to sign on? If possible, involve him or her at the very beginning. Your job should be less about convincing and more about engaging him or her to explore the Collaborative option with you. Ideally, it should at least seem that the idea has come from *both* of you.

If you need a refresher on some of the more compelling reasons to pursue the Collaborative approach, here's a list to share in your conversations with your spouse:

- The two of you are in control of the outcome and have ultimate veto power on the issues
- The time the process takes depends on the parties' timetable—you will set the pace of action for yourselves

- It generally costs less than traditional methods
- It takes the specific interests of both parties into consideration
- Collaborative lawyers work for settlement and do not go to court—therefore, they do not approach the divorce process in an adversarial way
- The process makes it much easier for you and your spouse to maintain ongoing relationships with your extended families
- It keeps your children out of the crossfire and keeps the crossfire to a minimum

Share Written Information

You may find it easier to give your spouse some reading material than to try to explain the smart divorce in your own words. This book, of course, is an excellent resource and we encourage you to share it or buy an extra copy for your spouse.

If you've already met with a Collaborative lawyer, he or she probably will have some brochures or other information that you can pass on to your spouse. In addition, the IACP (www.Collaborativepractice.com or 415-897-2398) and your local Collaborative group (located through the same Web site and phone number) both have excellent materials on Collaborative divorce available for free. Finally, if you see any news stories about Collaborative divorce in popular magazines or newspapers, you might want to clip them out and share them with your spouse.

Enrolling the Help of Clergy or Counselors

If you feel your spouse might not be receptive to a direct approach from you, think about whether there's a minister, priest,

GETTING YOUR SPOUSE TO AGREE

rabbi, psychologist, or good mutual friend who might be willing to learn enough about Collaborative law to be able to talk to your spouse about it.

Sarah, the wife of a prominent architect, had been thinking of a divorce for some time. She finally took the big step of calling Stu for an initial consultation. After a thorough review of her options, Sarah expressed a strong preference for the Collaborative method, so Stu advised her that both she and her husband, Arnold, would have to agree to retain Collaborative lawyers.

Sarah explained that Arnold had an angry, contentious disposition and probably wouldn't be receptive to any proposal she came up with. Stu suggested that Sarah approach a third party, such as a minister, psychologist, or good friend of Arnold's about talking with him about the Collaborative approach, but Sarah couldn't think of anyone appropriate. Finally, Stu offered to write a letter to Arnold stating that Sarah had been in to see him, describing the Collaborative process, and inviting Arnold to contact Stu if he might be interested in participating in this type of a divorce process. Sarah agreed. Two days later, Arnold surprised Sarah by calling Stu and expressing his interest in Collaborative law. He even asked Stu for the names and phone numbers of a few Collaborative attorneys as referrals. Arnold retained one of these lawyers, and Sarah ultimately was pleased with their very successful Collaborative divorce.

Enlisting Your Attorney to Write a Letter to Your Spouse

Finally, most attorneys would be willing to write a letter to your spouse explaining the process. (See Appendix C for a sample letter.) Stu once wrote such a letter on behalf of a wife seeking Collaborative representation.

The lawyer you have contacted might be willing, even at this early stage, to meet with you and your spouse to describe the process—without dealing at all with the issues of your particular situation.

Your spouse needs to know that he or she needs to retain a Collaborative lawyer in order to pursue this process. If your spouse retains a non-Collaborative lawyer you won't be able to utilize the Collaborative method.

Do You Need to Hire an Attorney?

Obviously, if you're considering having your lawyer write your spouse a letter or meet your spouse, you're planning on hiring an attorney. There are many excellent reasons to do so, though there have been couples throughout our tenure as divorce lawyers who've asked if lawyers are necessary, particularly in a Collaborative situation.

Technically, you and your spouse can get a legal divorce without either of you seeking or securing representation. If you've worked out everything to your mutual satisfaction, you can complete the process using standardized forms that are widely available online or at your courthouse. However—and this is a *big* however—we strongly recommend that you hire a lawyer at least in an advisory capacity. (If you have children and/or substantial assets, trying to go it alone is a risky proposition, and we believe that you and your spouse should both have lawyers.)

First, the emotionality of divorce makes it difficult to make sound decisions without professional advice. Second, the do-it-yourself forms can be extremely complicated and many nonlawyers find the process of filling them out overwhelming. Third, having an attorney look over your paperwork can help you identify areas you may have overlooked as well as any potential legal problems that your agreements may inadvertently raise. Naturally, you're free to take or leave the lawyer's advice as it suits you.

In most jurisdictions it would be unethical for one lawyer to represent both you and your spouse, as you don't necessarily have the same interests.

Coordinating Your Attorney Search with Your Spouse

If your spouse has already agreed to use the Collaborative process, we suggest that the two of you begin your search together. This will help you find attorneys with similar approaches and, if possible, attorneys who have worked together successfully in the past. It may seem odd that we would recommend finding attorneys who have worked well together in the past. Outside of the Collaborative process, there is a tendency to be suspicious of attorneys who are too "friendly" for fear that they will not work aggressively enough to protect their clients' interests. In the Collaborative process, we have found the opposite to be true. We can do a better job helping a client achieve his or her interests if their spouse is represented by a skilled Collaborative attorney that we know and respect.

In Collaborative cases, your ability to get the best possible outcome will not depend on your attorney's ability to gain a strategic "edge" over the other attorney but rather on the ability of all participants to create an environment in which the best win-win options are discovered.

You may even consider interviewing attorneys together if the attorneys you are considering are willing to meet with the both of you. (Some choose not to do so, out of concern that it could create

Alan and Nancy had been married for eighteen years and had two children, Jason, age twelve, and Sara, age nine. Nancy had been unhappy in the marriage since the beginning, but had never wanted to consider divorce. Alan admitted that there had been problems in the marriage, but he believed that Nancy blew these things out of proportion. "All couples have these kinds of issues," he insisted.

Over the years Alan and Nancy had been to a marriage counselor and, on occasion, things would improve. However, the problems eventually would reappear and new ones cropped up along the way. For many years Nancy had been frustrated by the fact that Alan was often consumed with his work and did not spend enough time with the family. There would often be brief periods when things got better, but then Alan would slide back into his old habits. Their discussions about Alan's work hours often turned into heated arguments, and their ability to communicate with each other, once a strong point in their marriage, steadily deteriorated. Finally, after a long and bitter argument about Alan's failure to come home in time for their son, Jason's, ninth birthday party, Nancy decided she was tired of fighting to save the marriage. She knew that a divorce was necessary, but she wanted to minimize the impact on the children.

Nancy had learned about Collaborative law through her sister and decided to meet with a Collaborative attorney to find out more. She left the meeting convinced that this was the best approach for them, but she had doubts about whether Alan would cooperate.

Two nights later, she told Alan that she was filing for a divorce and that she wanted to use the Collaborative method. As she feared, Alan was so upset he wouldn't even discuss a Collaborative approach. In fact, he threatened to hire an aggressive attorney to "take the kids from her." Later on, he changed his position and said he wouldn't hire an attorney at all since he thought all of them were "sleazy."

Nancy thought she'd have to abandon her hope for a Collaborative divorce and was ready to hire a traditional attorney just to move forward. However, after talking with her attorney and considering her options, she decided to hold off on filing papers for a few months, with the hope that over time Alan might be able to accept the idea of the divorce and would agree to consider the Collaborative approach.

To Nancy's delight, Alan did eventually come around. Once it became clear to Alan that the divorce was going to happen whether he liked it or not, he agreed to look into the Collaborative method. Nancy's attorney recommended a few attorneys and eventually Alan hired one.

Nancy was amazed to see how smoothly the process proceeded once they finally got to the first four-way meeting. While it was obvious that Alan still wished the divorce weren't happening, it was clear that he was starting to see how working together was in everyone's best interests—especially their children's. They were able to work out a full agreement within four months.

In addition, the managed negotiations during the Collaborative process actually helped Nancy and Alan regain some of their ability to communicate in a respectful and effective manner, particularly on issues affecting their children. This helped them work through many decisions in the years following the divorce.

a conflict of interest.) One advantage of coordinating your attorney selection with your spouse is that it can help build trust between the two of you and among the four of you. In a traditional divorce, it's common for both spouses to fear that the other's attorney will be maneuvering for his or her client's advantage. But in the Collaborative process, the two attorneys work together as problem solvers.

As Collaborative attorneys, spouses of our clients frequently ask us to give them names of attorneys we recommend. We generally provide them with a long list, but sometimes they want a specific recommendation. To people who are unfamiliar with the Collaborative process, the idea that one party in a divorce would trust the other's lawyer to recommend an attorney is completely insane. However, the reality is that in each of these instances we recommend the same people we would for our best friends. We know that when we're working with a skilled Collaborative attorney we can do a much better job helping our clients achieve their goals.

The Three Stages of Choosing an Attorney

A thorough investigation into choosing an attorney generally will include the following phases:

1. Identifying candidates
2. Investigating prospective attorneys through written information
3. Interviewing prospective attorneys

Identifying Candidates

The three most common ways of locating Collaborative attorneys are:

- Asking others for recommendations
- Searching for attorneys through the Internet, Yellow Pages, and magazines
- Contacting legal associations, specialty groups, and referral services

ASKING OTHERS FOR RECOMMENDATIONS

The most natural place to start is by asking other people who have been through a divorce—especially anyone who's gone through a Collaborative divorce—to tell you about their experience with their attorney. In addition, if you have any personal relationships with attorneys in your community, ask them to recommend a Collaborative family-law attorney.

The number of Collaborative attorneys you'll have access to depends on where you live. In some communities, there are hundreds. However, while the number of Collaborative attorneys is increasing rapidly, there are still some communities without any.

What to Do If You Can't Find a Collaborative Attorney in Your Area

If you're unable to find a Collaborative attorney in your area, you may need to look for an attorney in a nearby community. Unlike traditional law, in which knowledge of local courts is essential, there is little harm in selecting an attorney from outside your immediate area, so long as your attorney is licensed to practice law in the state or province where you live.

Almost every state in the United States and every province of Canada now has attorneys who are trained in the Collaborative method. However, if you happen to live in one of the few states that do not yet have Collaborative attorneys, you may want to look for an attorney in a nearby state. For this to work, your Collaborative attorney may need to help you locate an attorney in your community who can act as "local counsel" so that your Collaborative attorney can represent you. The local attorney will make sure that all local laws and procedures in your jurisdiction are followed while the outside Collaborative attorney will help you resolve all of the issues in your case.

A FAST WAY TO IDENTIFY COLLABORATIVE ATTORNEYS IN YOUR AREA

If no one you know can recommend a Collaborative attorney, another excellent resource is the International Academy of

Collaborative Professionals (IACP). You can get referrals to local Collaborative attorneys and groups at the IACP's Web site (www.Collaborativepractice.com) or by phone at 415-897-2398. If neither of these organizations can refer you to Collaborative attorneys in your area, ask whether there have been any recent Collaborative-practice trainings in your area. There's always a chance that a group is being formed in your community but hasn't yet hit the IACP's databases.

Investigating Prospective Attorneys

Once you've identified several Collaborative attorneys in your area, the next step is to find the best one for you. You can do this by:

- Reading what is available to the public regarding that attorney
- Asking the attorney to send some information
- Interviewing the attorney

You can learn a great deal about your prospective attorneys through Web sites, articles, advertisements, attorney profiles on organizational Web sites, local magazines that occasionally feature area attorneys, and so on. This information may help you to learn about each candidate's location, experience, training, and hourly rates. You won't make your final decision based on this information, but it may help you narrow your search.

Once you've learned as much as you can through public information, contact the offices of some of the prospective attorneys and ask them to send information that isn't available otherwise. You'll probably get additional details about the size of the attorney's office, availability of support staff, and philosophy. You might also ask to see a standard fee agreement, which will give you a better idea of how much you can expect to pay.

After you've put together a short list of candidates, schedule some interviews.

Interviewing Prospective Attorneys

There's a lot to be said for chemistry, and since you and your attorney will be working closely together on a very important decision in your life, it's important that you feel that he or she is someone you trust and are comfortable with. Interviews are also a way to get a better sense of an attorney's style, organization habits, enthusiasm for your Collaborative case, and clarity in explaining options.

Ideally, your interview should be in person. However, if circumstances only allow a phone interview, that will have to do. Either way, before setting up the interview, you should be clear in your own mind why you're calling. Is the interview only to help you make a hiring decision? Is it to have someone explain your options? Or is it to try to get some specific legal advice about your case? Many attorneys will provide brief informational interviews or explain your options (Collaborative law, mediation, litigation) for free, but it may well be worth paying a fee for a longer, more detailed session. And if you're seeking legal advice, we can almost guarantee that the attorney will charge you. We suggest that you *not* seek any legal advice in your first meeting, since it will probably be too short for the attorney to have the information he or she needs to really address your specific situation. For a checklist of possible questions to ask your attorney during your interview, see Appendix D.

Making Comparisons and Making a Final Decision

Consider the following in preparing for your research and/or interview:

Cost

Although a Collaborative divorce generally is cheaper than a traditional one, it still can seem relatively expensive if you're on a tight budget. Try to find out as much as you can about the financial side of things so that you won't be surprised, but understand that it's not easy for any attorney to accurately estimate the total cost of your case. One of the advantages of a Collaborative divorce is that the costs are almost entirely dictated by how long it takes you and your spouse to reach an agreement on all your issues. But since you don't know how long that will be, your attorney can't know either. So getting a firm dollar figure is nearly impossible.

Divorce attorneys bill by the hour and generally charge a *retainer*, which is a payment made at the beginning of your relationship. The retainer is applied toward the initial work on your case. Almost all attorneys use a written retainer agreement, which is a written contract that describes their billing policies and the financial terms of their representation, including how many hours the retainer covers. Review this contract carefully so you fully understand it. The Collaborative process as it pertains to you and your spouse is based on principles of transparency and integrity—these same principles apply to the contract between you and your attorney. It is important that you have confidence in your attorney for your relationship to run smoothly.

Be careful not to assume that the total cost of your divorce will be directly related to the attorney's hourly rate. Attorneys' rates are usually tied to their experience level, and one with more experience may be able to handle certain tasks more quickly than another with less experience. For example, an attorney who charges $250 per hour but can draft a certain document in two hours is ultimately less expensive than one who charges $175 per hour but needs three hours to prepare the same document.

Whether you will need a more experienced attorney depends on the specifics of your case. If you have complex assets or a complicated child-custody situation, you'll probably save money in the long run by hiring someone with a lot of experience in those areas. On the other hand, if your case does not seem to present complex issues, you may be better served with a less experienced attorney who charges a lower hourly rate and is more accessible.

If you are concerned about whether the hourly rates charged by the attorneys that you interview are reasonable, you can review the profiles in the Collaborative law Web sites in your area to get a sampling of hourly rates that are common in your community. However, if you do this, keep in mind that differences in hourly rates generally are related to the experience levels of the attorneys you are researching.

Experience and Training

In choosing a Collaborative attorney, your main focus should be on settlement skills, in particular, the type of interest-based negotiation skills taught in Collaborative and mediation trainings. However, since most Collaborative attorneys also do some courtroom work (in other areas), they'll generally have some litigation experience.

For the purposes of a Collaborative divorce, your prospective attorney's litigation background is far less important than his or her other experience—but it's not irrelevant. In fact, it could be very important—positively or negatively. Some people believe that an

Retainer Agreements

You hire an attorney by signing a *retainer agreement*. While each lawyer drafts his or her own, most retainer agreements include the following topics:

1. A statement indicating that your Collaborative lawyer will represent you for settlement, but will withdraw from the case if the matter becomes adversarial or requires court proceedings
2. The lawyer's hourly rate and a listing of any additional items that may be billed separately
3. The amount of the retainer. When you write a check for the retainer, you're actually paying in advance for a certain number of hours at the lawyer's standard rate

Because the retainer agreement outlines the terms of your relationship with your attorney, we suggest that you take it home with you and read it carefully. If you have any questions or concerns, ask them *before* signing the document. Some retainer agreements state that the attorney can keep any unused portion of the retainer fee if your case takes less time to resolve than anticipated or if the attorney withdraws from the case. You may want to have that clause *taken out* before you sign the agreement. Generally, retainer balances should be returned to you, regardless of the reason.

attorney's litigation background helps with Collaborative cases, since it provides a better context in which to assess your full range of choices. On the other hand, attorneys with a great deal of litigation experience may have trouble unlearning old habits and can, on occasion, slide into a litigation frame of mind. In evaluating a prospective attorney's experience, you may want to consider the following:

- General family law experience
- Experience and training in Collaborative law
- Experience and training in mediation
- Experience in working with your spouse's attorney

The most important attribute to look for may be experience and training in Collaborative cases. However, because Collaborative law is still relatively new, it is possible that your attorney may not have handled many Collaborative cases despite having a long and successful law career. That's not necessarily a bad thing. There are many cases in which a less experienced attorney with a lower hourly rate could be the best fit for you. In addition, there are always examples of attorneys whose broad life experience and other training may allow them to become excellent Collaborative attorneys in a short period of time.

Experience and training in mediation are valuable in that many of the skills and principles of mediation are similar to the skills used in Collaborative practice. Many Collaborative groups require their attorneys also to be trained in mediation.

Full-time Collaborators

A small minority of attorneys devote their full practice to out-of-court solutions, such as Collaborative law and mediation. Whether there are advantages to having an attorney who works exclusively in the area of Collaborative law is a matter of personal opinion. On the one hand, someone who practices Collaborative law exclusively will likely have a high level of experience, and there is little danger of him or her slipping into an adversarial pattern. However, there are many experienced Collaborative attorneys who are outstanding in their Collaborative work despite working both in and out of court.

After twenty-seven years of marriage, Greg, age forty-eight, and Ann, age forty-seven, agreed to file for divorce. They had really drifted apart during the prior ten years, and they were both aware of the fact that, to some extent, they had stayed together for the sake of the children. Now with one daughter in college and the other in her senior year in high school, Greg and Ann agreed that it was time to end the marriage.

They both felt they could work out most of the issues on their own and, for a while, wondered whether they even needed attorneys. However, because Greg seemed to have a better handle on the finances, Ann was concerned that she needed some protection to make sure they reached a settlement that would allow her to meet her financial needs throughout the rest of her life. Greg understood her concerns but had heard too many stories about how couples wound up fighting once the attorneys explained their "rights" to them.

Ann found out about the Collaborative process through a friend, and she thought that it would get her the protection she needed without allowing the attorneys to "take over." When she mentioned it to Greg, he liked the concept but was still concerned that having lawyers, even Collaborative lawyers, would cause them to fight over issues they seemed to be keeping in proper perspective. They both agreed to interview some attorneys together to help them decide. After looking through some biographical information on their local Collaborative practice Web site, they selected three attorneys to interview.

All three were trained in the Collaborative method and said that they would be committed to helping them settle the case. However, it seemed clear to Greg that one of the attorneys was less likely to let them do it their way. This particular attorney didn't seem to be listening as much as the other two and spoke more about each of their "rights" than about their concerns. Greg really felt that this lawyer might easily drift into arguing for his client under the belief that he was simply protecting his or her "rights."

Greg and Ann decided on the two other attorneys and the process went quite smoothly. Ironically, as it turned out, it was Greg's attorney who wound up cautioning Greg that the property settlement he was agreeing to probably was more generous than one that might have been decided by a court. However, the attorney did not pressure Greg to seek a different settlement, and a full agreement was reached with very little turmoil.

Colleen and Phil had no difficulty agreeing on the Collaborative process. It made a great deal of sense to both of them. However, Colleen really struggled to find an attorney that seemed like the right match. She had interviewed five (two by phone only) and felt that they all had different strengths. Oddly enough, the one that her "gut instinct" favored was Linda, the least experienced attorney of the group. Although Linda had only been practicing for three years and had been a Collaborative attorney for less than a year, Colleen really liked Linda's enthusiasm for the Collaborative process and felt that Linda had listened to her more than the others. During the interview, Linda, unlike any of the other attorneys, put down her pen, made eye contact, and was completely focused during the meeting. Colleen followed her instinct and hired Linda to represent her. It worked out even better than Colleen had imagined. Linda did a great job helping Colleen identify her goals and explaining her options. Colleen and Phil's case was not terribly complicated from a financial standpoint, so Linda's relative inexperience was never an issue.

Perhaps the safest thing to say is that if your attorney spends a great deal of time in court, try to satisfy yourself that he or she is committed enough to the Collaborative practice to properly guide you through the process.

Gender

Occasionally, clients believe that it's important to have an attorney of their gender (or the opposite gender). There is no research to support either theory, and we haven't even seen any anecdotal evidence that an attorney's gender matters at all. However, if *you* are going to feel uncomfortable working with a person of a particular gender, go with the attorney who makes you feel most at ease.

Occasionally, clients will choose a lawyer of a particular gender based on their perceptions of how their spouse reacts to that gender. While knowing how your spouse will react in certain situations sometimes can be helpful, we've found that when it comes to gender, this kind of speculation is usually unreliable. The relationship between a Collaborative attorney and a Collaborative client is quite different than other relationships that you and your spouse have encountered. Your guess about how your spouse may relate to a Collaborative attorney of a particular gender is likely to be based on observations of relationships of a very different nature.

Location

If you are fortunate enough to have numerous attorneys in your area, you may want to consider geographic proximity. Several of our clients have picked attorneys whose offices were near their own or the other attorney's office, simply because they knew they'd be spending a significant amount of time there. Convenience, of course, is nice, but don't let it trump more significant concerns such as your general comfort level with a particular attorney and the level of the attorneys' experience and training in Collaborative practice. It may be worth traveling a distance to find a skilled practitioner who matches your particular personality.

Personality Match

As previously mentioned, when it comes to picking an attorney, chemistry is paramount. That's why it's especially important to try to meet with each prospective attorney in person—even if it's for only a few minutes. Many attorneys are willing to have a brief office meeting at no charge.

Philosophy

Your attorney's philosophy in handling family-law cases is an important factor in determining whether the attorney-client relationship will be a successful and productive one. While Collaborative attorneys have similar philosophies, we're certain that you will find enough individual variation to allow you to make a meaningful choice. You can determine an attorney's philosophy in a variety of ways, including in-person interview, Web site review, recommendations from friends or other attorneys, and/or any other written material you may have access to.

Working with Attorneys Who Have Worked with Each Other

One of the great advantages of searching for attorneys with your spouse is that you'll have a better chance of finding two who have worked together in the past. We have even seen couples who go out and interview attorneys together, with the idea that they will ultimately decide, as a couple, not only whom to hire, but which attorney will work with which client. This type of coordination reinforces the team approach from the very beginning.

Things You May Want to Learn About Your Attorney

After examining the factors outlined above and considering your specific needs, you may already know exactly what you want to ask prospective attorneys during your interviews. While the Collaborative process is primarily about you and your family (and less about the attorneys), it is still important to pick an attorney whom you can trust to give you guidance where it is needed. It is important that

We have worked "together" (meaning we have represented opposite sides in the same divorce) on a number of Collaborative cases. One of those cases involved Ben and Karen, both of whom were highly educated professionals who had three children, Susan, age fourteen, Bill, age eleven, and Jimmy, age six. Ben, represented by Ron, was a very successful oral surgeon, and earned a high income, while Karen, represented by Stu, was a CPA who had chosen to leave her employment and stay home for ten years while their children went through preschool.

At the time of the divorce, Karen was planning to reenter the work force but wanted to phase back into her career over a period of years. The parties experienced some tension, particularly on the issue of money. Because Ron and Stu have worked together a number of times, they had developed a level of trust between them that helped them sort out the valid financial issues from the emotional ones. They could talk about these issues openly during the four-way conferences without concern that either of them would raise false issues to create unnecessary conflict. Because the two attorneys knew each other well, they were able to create an atmosphere of transparency that assured both clients that all of the relevant facts had been disclosed and discussed.

you feel comfortable with your attorney so that you can express all of your concerns comfortably, regardless of the emotions that may be attached to them. It is also important that you feel confident that your attorney is truly hearing those concerns.

Selecting the right attorney will make your experience of the Collaborative process much more satisfying and much more productive, so take as much time as you need to make the best choice. And the addition of other professionals to your Collaborative team can make the difference between a relatively smooth journey and a rocky one. Chapter 4 provides the guidelines on just who else you may want to hire, in addition to your attorney, and why.

CHAPTER 4

Other Professionals You May Want on Your Divorce Team

Creating a Collaborative Team

Now that you and your spouse have retained your lawyers, it's time to consider adding other trained professionals to your Collaborative team. While some Collaborative lawyers prefer to work alone (which we professionals call the "lawyer-only model"), more and more are becoming open to working with other professionals from different disciplines, such as Collaborative coaches, neutral financial specialists, and neutral child specialists.

Each member of a typical Collaborative team plays his or her own individual role:

Collaborative lawyers act as educators and guides throughout the Collaborative and settlement process. They educate you about the process, explain the underlying legal rules and implications, and help frame the issues that are specific to your situation. They also play a major role in managing conflict as you move through the process, for example, by insisting on adherence to the ground rules and the terms of the Participation Agreement, reframing potentially hostile-sounding statements, working to maintain a favorable four-way settlement climate, and playing a key role in assisting with the negotiations.

Rebecca, thirty-one, and Steven, thirty-four, have been married for eight years. Their marriage has been characterized by a barrage and counterbarrage of negative name-calling and put-downs. They've lost the motivation to sustain the marriage to the negativity of their day-to-day put-downs. While they have had some marriage counseling, they've never been able to break their negative patterns.

Rebecca and Steven finally have arrived at the conclusion that they can't save the marriage. But it appears they are carrying their acrimony into the divorcing process. They have no children, but both have developed start-up companies, each of which has a fair market value estimated in the seven figures. They have kept their respective finances separate during the marriage. Perhaps instinctively to make the divorce easier, they have chosen to work with Collaborative professionals. The Collaborative lawyers they have retained have a strong bias toward encouraging the parties to develop a Collaborative team of professionals to work with them. In this case the parties agreed to select separate Collaborative coaches to help them move through the process more smoothly.

This decision was reinforced in the minds of their attorneys when an initial meeting between the attorneys and the parties turned into a vicious and angry verbal exchange between the parties. The lawyers apprised the coaches of the situation. As a result, the two lawyers and the two coaches met with Rebecca and Steven and explained to them that before work could begin with the attorneys to resolve their divorce issues, the parties needed to do some work with their coaches to make the settlement process possible. After much discussion and some resistance, the parties acknowledged their negative patterns and expressed a willingness to work on them with the coaches.

Over the next six weeks, the coaches met with the parties, separately at first and later as a couple. They helped the couple see their destructive behaviors and had them practice new ways of working with their feelings and communicating with their spouse. The coaches kept the attorneys aware of the progress. In the seventh week, it was decided to have a first definitive meeting of the attorneys with the parties.

For the first hour, it was agreed that the coaches would attend. The attorneys were literally astounded as to the changes in the behavior of the parties. Much progress was made toward settlement in this first session. The parties continued to meet with their coaches, but no major negative flare-up occurred during subsequent meetings. The parties have slowed down the pace of their meetings and rumor has it that Rebecca and Steven have been "dating" and talking tentatively about getting back together.

The attorneys also draft the documents and other paperwork to finalize the divorce with the court when agreement has been reached.

Collaborative coaches, or divorce coaches, are licensed mental-health professionals who are there to help you and your spouse (each one of you will have your own coach) handle emotional and psychological issues that might otherwise get in the way of the settlement process. They do *not* act as therapists. They can help you to prioritize issues, support you through the pain of loss and separation, work with you to improve communication patterns between you and your spouse, and help the whole Collaborative team identify and address potential obstacles to settlement. When appropriate, the two coaches and their clients may meet to address mutual concerns or facilitate the communication process.

Divorce coaches are vital members of the team. We estimate that only about 20 percent of what we deal with in a divorce matter is legal—the remaining 80 percent is emotional. Having coaches on the team allows the lawyers to stay centered on what we know best—the law and reaching mutually satisfactory settlements.

If you are interested in working with a coach, your attorney can help you select a coach that best fits your situation. In addition, one of the Collaborative law Web sites in your area is likely to list the coaches that are available in your community and to provide profiles for the coaches. It is often a good idea to interview two or more coaches to make sure you find one who is a good fit for you.

Child specialists are professionals trained and experienced in working with children, parents, and families in transition. As advocates for the children, they remain absolutely neutral in their relationship with the parents, talking directly with the children, who then have an opportunity to express their concerns if they are old enough to communicate clearly. The specialist makes recommendations to parents based on input from the children and also works with the parents to help them understand child-development stages and to develop a workable parenting plan. In our experience, this is the *only* divorce process that provides children a voice in shaping these plans—or even a chance to be heard in any significant way.

Financial specialists are neutral members of the team whose function is to help you and your lawyers assemble, organize, analyze, and understand your financial situation and the various options it offers. A typical financial specialist who's part of a Collaborative team will be skilled in determining personal net worth and budgeting, identifying tax laws that are relevant to the parties' situation, working with spousal maintenance issues, property valuations, and cash flow concerns. He or she will educate you and your spouse about money matters and, with approval of both parties, can meet with you individually if you need more education on basic financial issues, such as budgeting or checkbook maintenance.

Brenda and Roger are the parents of one child, a four-year-old named Barry. The parties are in the early stages of a Collaborative divorce, precipitated by Roger announcing that he is gay. They chose to form a full team of Collaborative professionals, including Sue, a fully qualified and trained child specialist. One of the issues between the parties was the involvement of each with their son, Barry, who has some pretty intensive learning disabilities and may be autistic. As a result of these disabilities, Brenda has taken over the management of Barry's development. Although she was doing this out of loving concern and not with an intent to exclude Roger, that was the result Roger perceived.

Sue interacted with Barry twice, and she talked with other professionals who knew the boy. One bit of information she gleaned from Barry was that he missed having more time with his dad.

When Sue met with the parents to give them her parenting recommendations, she was able to accurately report Barry's feelings and recommended that a strong effort be made to adjust their schedules to allow Roger more time with his son. Sue was able to do this in such a way that it served as a wake-up call for both parents. She kept the parties' coaches apprised of her recommendations so that they could reinforce the suggestions and help with their implementation. The coaches were also able to help the parties accept Roger's sexual orientation. Over a five-month period, the parties not only developed a new parenting schedule, giving Roger more time with Barry, but also made arrangements for Roger to take on the management of some of Barry's treatments that fall on Roger's time with Barry. This has relieved Brenda of shouldering all of these obligations and provided Roger with more loving responsibility for his son's well-being.

While this was not a situation Roger or Brenda would have wished for, in the end they have handled it with a fair amount of grace and integrity.

Neutral experts are commonly hired on an as-needed basis to perform specific jobs. For example, if you and your spouse own a business, you might need to retain a business valuation expert to determine its worth. Other neutral experts include real estate appraisers, mortgage consultants, and bankruptcy attorneys.

Why is neutrality important? It's best explained by considering what typically happens in litigation when an issue that requires an outside expert's opinion comes up. What often happens in that case is that each party hires his or her own separate expert to give an opinion in the matter. The result is more polarization, with the experts tending to tweak their opinions to favor the view of their client (who, of course, is paying them). Consider the following example:

Sally and Tom are divorcing after eighteen years of marriage; they have two children, ages fourteen and eight. Sally is initiating the divorce based on her belief that Tom will always be a workaholic, preferring his job to a relationship with Sally and the children. Sally knows Tom is a good provider but feels there is more to life than what she characterizes as being a "kept" woman.

Sally has served divorce papers on Tom and the matter is in litigation. One of the issues being debated is the value of the couple's home. Sally is currently living in the home with their children. She has indicated that she'd like to keep the house as part of the final division of assets.

A key factor in determining the final asset division is the fair-market value of the home. If the home is worth $500,000 and there is a $200,000 mortgage, the value of the home, after deducting the mortgage balance, would be $300,000. In a normal asset division, to keep the home Sally would have to pay Tom half of the $300,000 by allocating an additional $150,000 in other marital assets to Tom. But if the house was worth only $430,000, then by deducting the mortgage balance of $200,000 the "net" value of the home would be $230,000 and Sally would only owe Tom $115,000 rather than $150,000.

So Sally and her attorney hire an appraiser. She's obviously hoping for a lowball figure so that she'll owe Tom less if she ends up keeping the home. The expert in this case undoubtedly will try his best to accurately appraise the home. But the appraiser knows he was hired by Sally, who wants to keep the home, and when it comes time to come up with a final figure he may feel the need to provide the answer that Sally is seeking. So the resulting appraisal may be on the low side of the value range.

Tom, of course, hires a different appraiser to value the home. His appraiser knows that if Sally keeps the home Tom will be paid more or less for the home depending on the appraised value. Tom will be at the home to help highlight its positive points to the appraiser, with the hope that the appraisal ends up on the high side.

At trial, the judge will be confronted with conflicting home values. Which appraiser will the judge believe, or will he split the difference? And if the competing numbers are too far apart, might he order a third appraisal?

This is exactly the kind of situation you can avoid by using neutral experts. If a divorcing couple needs an appraiser, we ask our clients to agree on one from a list that we provide. Since the appraiser is working for *both* parties, he or she is under no pressure to color the report one way or the other. Appraisers love to work as neutrals for the very reason that they are free from the subtle pressures to favor the party who did the hiring and are able to do the best possible job.

In choosing an expert, the couple may agree in advance that they'll be bound by whatever the expert comes up with. Or they may agree that they'll want to preview the expert's report before agreeing to accept it. If they both agree to reject it, they'll need to come up with another appraiser and repeat the process.

Neutral experts are available to give opinions on a broad range of issues, from accounting and tax advising, residential real estate appraisals, commercial real estate appraisals, pension evaluations, classic car appraisals, personal property appraisals, jewelry appraisals, vocational counseling and evaluations, exotic animal appraisals, mortgage counseling and placement, parenting consulting, realty services, business valuations, and just about anything else you can think of. In short, if there's a product or service or asset or behavior that needs evaluating, there is a neutral expert who can get the job done!

Most of these experts do the job and are on their way. Financial specialists and child specialists—who have a more ongoing role in the Collaborative process and who may be involved from beginning to end and beyond—are the exceptions. For routine evaluations, the easiest way to choose a Neutral Expert is to take the recommendation of your Collaborative lawyers, who probably have worked with the expert in the past.

In other situations, you and your spouse might want to personally interview several candidates before jointly deciding on one. This is especially true if you're retaining a financial specialist or child specialist. The interviewing process should be personal and in-depth. You and your spouse should meet with the specialist together and compare notes afterward. You're going to have a very intimate relationship with this person, so he or she should be someone you trust and can get along with. In the case of child specialists, be sure to probe each candidate's views on child custody and parenting time to ensure that you are both comfortable hiring them.

Finally, the case manager is not an additional member of the team, but an already-existing team member who takes on this role to coordinate the team's activities and keeps everyone on task and accountable (much like a general contractor on a building renovation, whose job it is to keep the project on schedule).

Team or Consultants?

When you and your spouse bring in other professionals, in most cases it's as part of a team, meaning that all the players work together toward a common goal—resolving your divorce issues in a way that's beneficial to both you and your spouse. Team members work individually with you and communicate with each other when appropriate and needed. The more information each of the team's members has, the better the chance of reaching a positive outcome.

Each and every professional who has been discussed here in the framework of participating as part of a team also can be retained on an individual basis as a consultant. For example, instead of retaining a neutral financial person to work with you as a couple, you might hire a financial person to work with you individually. In that case, the financial expert would not be working with anyone but you and your attorney. While there are times when this might be useful, having team members working together oftentimes can be more powerful. Sharing information and expertise usually facilitates a better and smoother outcome.

Could coaches be useful in getting past your emotional traps? Could a child specialist give you better insight into the needs of your children? Might a financial specialist save you money by assembling your assets, helping with your budgets, and assisting with valuation of special assets, rather than having your attorneys do this (most likely at higher hourly rates)? You and your spouse should discuss with your lawyers the advantages of putting together a team of professionals for your particular situation.

Whether you choose consultants or decide to work only with your lawyers, you're ready to move to the four-way meeting, where the real action takes place and the decisions get made.

PART THREE

Getting Divorced, Collaboratively

PART THREE

CHAPTER 5

Four-Way Meetings

Outside of the Collaborative process the phrase "four-way meeting" could be used to describe any meeting of four people. However, when we use the phrase *Collaborative four-way meeting* in this book, we're referring to a specific type of meeting that typically involves four people, but sometimes more.

The Collaborative Four-Way Is Different from Other Four-Way Meetings

Settlement meetings between clients and their attorneys sometimes occur even in the traditional litigation approach to divorce. However, the rules and the style of these meetings are completely different from the Collaborative four-way meetings.

In many ways, your commitment to the Collaborative process will depend on the strength of your commitment to make these four-way meetings as effective as possible. They likely will be your greatest challenge, and they require much preparation. But they present unlimited opportunities to find solutions that will help you achieve your most important goals.

Although the analogy is often overused, the Collaborative process is similar to building a house. Your long-term goals and interests are the foundation. The more secure you are in the goals you have established, the more likely you are to achieve the successful and durable outcomes that you want.

Collaborative four-ways are like the frame of the house. Within that framework you will create the outcome that will make up your actual divorce agreement. The quality of the outcome likely will depend on the foundation and the framework that supports it.

One of the reasons it's valuable to compare the Collaborative process to the process of building a home is that it will prepare you to be patient during the early stages of the four-way meetings. Much of the time spent in these early meetings will be for the purpose of setting the foundation and framing the issues. During these early stages, you may find yourself tempted to want to jump ahead to final decisions before you are ready to do so. So please carefully read the sections that follow. We strongly believe that the better you understand how four-way meetings work, the more likely you will be able to use them effectively.

Practical Aspects of the Typical Collaborative Four-Way Meetings

Let's turn to the practical task of explaining what actually happens in these meetings:

- **Who** attends the meetings? Usually these meetings will include you, your spouse, and both attorneys.
- **Where** do these meetings take place? Generally at the offices (or conference rooms) of one of the attorneys.

- **When** do these meetings take place? They're generally scheduled about two to four weeks apart, at a time when all the participants can be there.
- **What** happens during these meetings? Typically:

  - **Introductions** are made and a **tone** is set for the meetings
  - **Ground rules** are established for how to conduct the meetings
  - The Collaborative process is explained and discussed
  - **Reasons for choosing** the Collaborative method are discussed
  - If it is the first meeting, the **Participation Agreement** is reviewed and signed.
  - **Goals** and **interests** are identified
  - **Information** is fully disclosed
  - **Issues and interests** are identified
  - **Questions** are answered
  - **Homework** is determined
  - Issues are **prioritized**
  - **Alternatives** are identified and evaluated
  - **Agreements** are reached
  - **Agendas** are set for future meetings
  - **Documents** are signed
  - Decisions are made about whether to include other **team members**
  - Decisions are made about whether to retain **experts**
  - **Final steps** for completing the process are outlined

The goals you establish and the critical interests you define in the early four-way meetings form the foundation for your success in this process.

Identifying Goals and Interests

All of the steps in the Collaborative process exist for one purpose: to help you achieve your most important legitimate goals. But you can't achieve them if you haven't first carefully considered what they are. There's a natural tendency to become absorbed in the immediate problems that you are facing and to focus only on narrow ideas about how you might resolve these urgent concerns. Your success in the Collaborative process will depend a great deal on your ability to pause in the middle of the chaos to truly think about your long-term goals. In chapter 7 and Appendix E we will give you a better understanding of what we mean by goals and interests, and provide examples of some common goals to guide you. Keeping these crucial goals in mind will make it easier to make compromises or let go of less significant issues in order to preserve the things that matter the most to you.

The other reason for you and your spouse to identify your overall goals is that you're likely to find that you share a number of them. Identifying these common interests will provide greater opportunities to find solutions for accomplishing these goals.

The Conflict-Resolution Process

The framework of Collaborative four-ways is generally developed around the following four steps:

1. Identifying issues
2. Gathering facts
3. Developing options
4. Negotiating solutions

Your attorney will explain to you why each of these stages is important and will help you avoid one of the most common mistakes that people in the Collaborative process make: skipping the preliminaries and jumping right into negotiating solutions.

Identifying Issues: You Can't Find the Answers Unless You Know the Questions

You may believe that you already know all the issues that you need to resolve, but chances are there are quite a few that would never occur to you unless you were a practicing Collaborative attorney. In addition, your list may not include concerns or issues that your spouse may have. Before you can begin working on any specific issue, it is important to identify as many as you can so you can get a better sense of how to prioritize the next steps.

To give you an example of the types of issues that often arise in divorce cases, review the list in Appendix E. While no list can be all-inclusive, these examples should give you a general feel for the types of issues that will need to be resolved.

Gathering Facts: Making Sure You Have All of the Pieces of the Puzzle

Once you have identified the issues, the next step is to gather information. You can't make good decisions unless you're confident that you have all of the information you need to do so. The Collaborative model uses an informal process that's designed to collect the facts as quickly and inexpensively as possible. During the four-way meetings the attorneys help the clients identify what kind of information they may need to help them make decisions. Generally, one or more of the participants will agree to take responsibility for obtaining the information, and the requested information is distributed to the other members of the group prior to the next four-way meeting.

Developing Options: Imagining the Unimaginable

Now you're ready to consider your alternatives. In many instances, you may believe you have already considered every possible way of resolving the issues at hand. However, if you spend time considering other possibilities, you'll be surprised at how many more you can generate.

Negotiating Solutions: Finding the Right Answers

If you've done a thorough job with the first three steps, you'll find it easy to negotiate workable solutions. If you reach an impasse in resolving any of the issues, your attorneys (and any other professionals who may be assisting you) will help you identify ways of getting around it.

Roles of the Parties and the Attorneys During the Four-Way Meeting

While you and your spouse are ultimately responsible for the outcomes of the four-way meetings, your attorneys are primarily responsible for keeping the process on track and for creating a safe and effective environment for reaching solutions. You and your spouse also play a role in creating and maintaining an environment that is conducive to problem solving.

Safe and Effective Environments

Safe Environment

While protection from harm or threats of harm is, of course, critical to the Collaborative process, our definition of *safe environment* goes well beyond physical safety. To ensure success in the Collaborative process, all participants need to work toward creating an environment in which:

- None of the participants feels frightened or intimidated
- None of the participants feels undue pressure to settle issues
- Each participant is able to express his or her interests
- Each participant is able to suggest possible solutions without fear of reprisal
- Each participant feels empowered to make important decisions
- Each participant avoids making accusations or attempting to assign blame
- None of the participants makes threats to go to court
- All participants are free to say "I don't know"
- All participants are free to take time to consider proposals
- All participants are free to object to behavior by other participants
- All participants feel heard
- All participants are able to take a break at any time
- All participants are respected
- All honest opinions are considered

Effective Environment

As important as a safe environment is, it can't produce success on its own. It's also essential that all participants work to create an environment that is *effective* in helping them meet their goals. An effective environment is one in which:

- All participants have access to the information they need to make decisions
- All participants understand what is being discussed
- The meeting stays on the agenda
- Each participant takes time to prepare for the meeting
- One participant makes a clear record of the discussions
- The meeting moves at a pace that is acceptable to everyone
- All participants work to separate emotional reactions from the decision-making process

Safe and Effective Two-Way Meetings

Early in the process, it often becomes evident that many tasks can be performed by the two clients on their own, outside of the four-way meetings. This can be advantageous because it can potentially save on legal fees and it can give the clients the opportunity to develop (or restore) trust and communication skills without outside influence. However, in order for these two-way meetings to work, it is important that you and your spouse are confident that you can create and maintain a safe and effective environment in which these meetings take place. Sometimes it is helpful to use the four-way meetings to plan your two-way meetings so that you can figure out how to make these meetings work best.

Addressing the Emotional and Financial Challenges of Four-Way Meetings

We feel confident that you will see just how effective four-way meetings can be if you choose to pursue a Collaborative divorce. However, your success in these meetings may depend on your ability to address the emotional and financial challenges that may arise.

The Emotional Challenge

Collaborative four-way meetings, while effective, can often be emotionally difficult. The thought of sitting in the same room as your spouse and his or her attorney might cause you a great deal of discomfort. If that's true, it's important that you communicate with your attorney, coach, or other professionals about your discomfort, so that they can help you develop specific strategies that will work for you.

Special Situations

There are some cases in which the emotional challenges are so great that special accommodations need to be made. If, for example, you and/or your spouse are having tremendous difficulty accepting the divorce, direct interaction with one another could trigger strong feelings that make it difficult to create a safe and effective environment during the four-way meetings. And certainly in cases where there has been a history of abuse or where there is a strong power imbalance, adjustments may need to be made, and it may not even be possible for the spouses to have direct interaction.

If you find your four-way meetings to be emotionally challenging, you and your attorney may want to consider the following options.

1. Add specific ground rules to ensure that discussions avoid triggering strong emotional responses.
2. Work with divorce coaches or divorce-closure counselors to do your part in creating a better environment.
3. Meet in two separate rooms for all or part of the four-way meetings and have the attorneys move back and forth between the two rooms. In these situations, the four-way

Meg and Marvin had a very rocky marriage—and it was beginning to look like their divorce would be the same, in spite of the fact that they had successfully formed a Collaborative team: two Collaborative lawyers, two coaches, a child specialist, and a financial neutral. While waiting for the first four-way meeting to start, Marvin was informed by Meg that he was going to be served with a legal restraining order—highly inappropriate behavior for a Collaborative proceeding. Apparently Meg and Marvin had argued about the divorce two nights earlier and Marvin had threatened to "get back" at Meg for filing for the divorce. Upset by Marvin's threat, Meg had seriously considered dropping the Collaborative process and seeking a restraining order—and though she ultimately decided not to, she mentioned it anyhow, elevating already-high tensions at the first four-way meeting. In fact, shortly after this exchange, Meg refused to be in the same room with Marvin.

Finally it was agreed that the divorce coaches would join the next four-way meeting so that the parties could work first on creating a safe environment. While the meetings were often difficult, Marvin and Meg eventually were able to reach an agreement. In addition, while their ability to communicate continued to be quite limited, they did develop some skills and techniques to allow them to communicate about the children without allowing the discussions to deteriorate into arguments or threats.

meetings are often replaced by three-way meetings, with the attorneys meeting with each client individually.

4. Slow down the process to allow the parties more time to make the emotional adjustment necessary for more effective four-way meetings.

5. Spend additional time preparing for these meetings with your attorneys and/or coaches.

Following these suggestions is not going to magically make your four-way meeting fun and enjoyable. Even in the best situations you'll probably feel a little uncomfortable. As a general rule, four-way meetings are hard work for all participants. However, in almost all cases, the benefits gained by directly participating in your solutions will justify your commitment and hard work.

The Financial Challenge

Much of the expense of your case will be related to these meetings. Your attorneys will spend time preparing for them, attending them, and summarizing or debriefing them. As a result, you may be worried about how much they're costing. If you're worrying about your bills, you're not going to be fully present for the meetings, and the meetings won't be nearly as effective. As with the emotional challenge, running from the problem may only make it worse, so it's important to address this financial challenge:

1. Read chapter 7 on the commitment needed for the Collaborative process and consider whether the amount you are spending will have an impact on the quality of your outcome.

2. Be as thorough as you can in gathering and organizing the information that you need for the meetings. This can reduce your legal fees dramatically in two ways: First, you avoid having your attorney charge you for doing legwork you could have done on your own. Second, the four-way meetings are more productive because all of the information you need is readily available and organized in a useful way.

3. Create a structure for safe and effective two-way meetings with your spouse so that you can address as many issues as possible outside the four-ways.
4. Talk with your attorney about how you can make the four-way meetings more effective.
5. Make sure that there is enough time between the four-way meetings so everyone is prepared. It can be tempting to rush the process by asking that meetings be scheduled close together. This may seem like a way of getting more done more quickly, but if busy schedules prevent the parties or the attorneys from completing the necessary homework between meetings, the four-ways will be less productive and more of them will be needed.
6. Finally, think about whether you need to let go of some smaller issues that could be bogging down the progress of the meetings. Even people who are very cost conscious can lose perspective and spend a disproportionate amount of time on minor issues. Between meetings, when there is time to reflect, think about whether the cost of holding onto that issue is really worth the resources and emotional energy that you are investing in it.

Although they had been married almost seventeen years, Wendy and David both expected their divorce would be fairly easy. They did not have children, so there were no custody or child support issues. They both had good jobs, so neither of them wanted alimony from the other. In fact, they had been separated for more than a year and had been paying their own expenses. Their marital estate primarily consisted of the equity in their house and their 401(k) accounts, and they were both content to divide those assets equally. They did not have significant debt and they both wanted to keep their attorneys' fees to a minimum so they would not leave the marriage in debt.

Their Collaborative divorce went fairly well, but it took them longer than they expected to reach an agreement, primarily because of difficulties that they had in dividing $8,000 in credit-card debt. Most of the difficulty centered around their joint Visa credit card that had a balance of approximately $3,500. David believed that balance should be divided equally, just like the rest of the debt. But Wendy felt that David should pay two-thirds of the Visa debt because he had incurred some of the debt on a vacation he had taken with his new girlfriend during the separation. David, who is self-employed as a marketing consultant, acknowledged that his girlfriend had accompanied him on the trip but insisted the trip was business-related, and that virtually all of the expenses were business costs.

Wendy was upset that David would try to get her to share in expenses that she felt were completely personal in nature. David felt that Wendy was "nitpicking" on this issue and that she was just trying to control him.

After several heated discussions about the topic, they decided to go through the credit card statements and receipts with their attorneys to separate out the business expenses from the personal expenses that David had incurred. After two meetings in which the Visa debt was the central issue, they ultimately agreed that David would pay an extra $800 of the Visa debt. While this solution had saved Wendy approximately $400, in the end, she was amazed to see that she had incurred more than $900 in fees working on this issue. David, in looking at his final fees, realized that it would have been cheaper for him to accept Wendy's original proposal. Both Wendy and David spent more money "resolving" this issue than they would have spent if they had found a way to let it go.

Four-way meetings are the building blocks of the Collaborative process. Successful four-way meetings can help you reach agreements that will allow both spouses to achieve their goals and create a groundwork for communication after the divorce. Now that you have an idea about how four-way meetings work, chapter 6 will explain how specific issues are handled through the Collaborative process.

CHAPTER 6

Addressing Specific Issues Via the Collaborative Process

While we obviously can't anticipate the issues that are unique and individual to your specific situation, we can provide some examples, based on our collective experience, of how we've handled difficult issues that commonly arise among divorcing couples. One caution: Ask your attorney to filter this information through the lens of the laws of your state. Remember, too, these examples are only some of the ways these issues can be handled.

Each of the sections below begins with a few examples of statements you might use to jump-start the discussion. These statements are worded in a way to encourage and facilitate discussion rather than stifle it.

The Marital Home

1. My goal is to be able to provide a stable, familiar environment for our children until our youngest child has turned eighteen.
2. My goal is for us to have enough financial liquidity to be able to provide similar and desirable facilities for ourselves and the children.

3. My interest is to explore all possible ways in which we can afford to maintain our home for a reasonable period of time.

You and your spouse will have to agree on what your home is currently worth. You then deduct the balance owed on all outstanding mortgages and lines of credit that use the home as collateral. There are several ways to arrive at a current home value.

- If you and your spouse are confident that you know what the house is worth, you simply can agree to use that value.
- If you're not sure of the value, you can rely on one or more neutral experts mentioned previously. Together you might ask two or more realtors who specialize in homes in your neighborhood to see the house and give you their opinions on its value. Realtors generally do not charge for this service and their opinions usually are informal, but some of our clients have opted for this approach since they felt that realtors are closest to the actual real-estate market.
- The most technical approach is to get the house appraised. A certified appraiser probably will charge you a few hundred dollars to do a formal, detailed, written appraisal of the property. Again, you and your spouse will have to agree on a neutral appraiser to use, and both of you should be present while the appraisal is done.

If, for example, the agreed-upon value of the home (what you could sell it for) is $500,000, and you owe a total of $300,000 in mortgages and home equity lines of credit, you and your spouse would technically make a profit off the difference ($200,000) if you sold the house. If the home was the only asset and one of you wanted to keep it, he or she would have to pay the other half of that amount, or $100,000, to buy the other person's interest in the property.

A lot of our clients initially say that they want the home as part of their share of the settlement. We suggest that, before getting too attached to that idea, you talk it over with your neutral financial person. Depending on your overall financial situation, it might not be as good an investment as it sounds. It's best to explore all options in the context of your entire settlement and the desirability of meeting all your goals, together with those of your spouse, when possible.

Time with the Children

Sample statements:

- My goal is to make the best interests of our children our primary focus.
- I want both of us to have the best possible relationships with each of our children.
- I want my time with the children to include quality "being-there" time and not just "Disney-parent" time.
- I want us to develop an increased ability to communicate with our children around their issues.
- I want us to work together with our children in such a way that they will feel able to include us both for special occasions.

When faced with child-sharing issues, the courts—and thus the parents—traditionally have used a lot of labels, such as *sole physical custody*, *joint physical custody*, *sole legal custody*, *joint legal custody*, and others. Often the amount of child support to be received or paid is inversely correlated to the amount of time the "noncustodial" parent spends with the children. As you can no doubt imagine, this is a source of endless courtroom battles.

So the question becomes, can we ignore the labels and just talk about how we're going to parent? Can we put together a parenting agreement that becomes part of our divorce? In some states, yes, you can prepare a parenting plan in lieu of custody designations. In others, state law may still require labels, but a parenting plan will help you both define your parenting time and obligations. If you're

Mary and Tom opted to include a neutral child specialist and a neutral financial specialist on their Collaborative team.

They are in their third four-way meeting, having met separately with both specialists. The child specialist has also met with their two children, Suzy, ten, and Ben, seven. During their marriage Tom was what might be termed the primary parent, handling most of the day-to-day routines with the children: getting them up on school days, making breakfast, and taking them to school. He is usually there when they return from school, or has made arrangements for them to go to a neighbor's. Tom has also taken care of most of the meals, laundry, family shopping, trips to the doctor, and driving to take the children to and from their many activities and lessons: dance, karate, hockey, soccer, and piano.

Mary is a successful entrepreneur, having built her business from scratch, from a one-woman operation to fifteen full-time employees. While she recognizes that Tom has done most of the day-to-day parenting of the children, she has also devoted a number of her evenings and weekends to spending time with the children: attending their activities, practicing piano with Ben, and helping both children with their homework.

The pending divorce has been a wake-up call for Mary. She wants a more involved relationship with the children and is willing to make drastic changes in her work patterns to achieve it. She would like to have an arrangement where the children spend half their time with her, and, as such, she intends to purchase a home in the same school district within a mile from the couple's current home. Mary even acknowledges that there is a lot she needs to learn about parenting, and has enrolled in a parenting-skills class.

The child specialist has spent time with both children. It's clear from his reports that the children love both of their parents and would like to spend more time with their mother if possible. The child specialist also met with both parents on several occasions, shared with them his recommendations, and discussed each parent's viewpoints on the issue.

Tom has a lot of ambivalence about spending less time with the children and is concerned about whether Mary is up to the task of frequent full-time mother. On the other hand, he also looks forward to the possibility of having a respite from full-time responsibility for the children.

After much discussion back and forth, the parties agreed that, until Mary purchases her new home, the children would spend every other weekend with Mary at her apartment complex. They also agreed that Mary would assume half of the duties Tom currently has in transporting the children, and that she will be on call if Tom should need her to be with the children after school. If this works well, the parties will work out a 50-50 time-sharing arrangement that they would try for a six-month period once Mary is in her new home. The child specialist gave his approval to the proposal, indicating that he would be available to work with the parties and the children to get beyond any speed bumps that may arise.

Tom, Mary, the child specialist, and both attorneys then drafted a Parenting Plan, which detailed their agreements around sharing time with the children. What still remains to be discussed is a plan to ensure that after the divorce Tom, Mary, and their children are all as financially secure as possible.

interested in developing a parenting plan, your attorneys and neutral child specialists can help you craft one. (See also the parenting guidelines in Appendix F.)

Don't be afraid to try out some unfamiliar routines in shaping your time-sharing plan. Everything is going to be different after the divorce: your family structure, your households, perhaps even your jobs or schools. You or your spouse may be taking on new parenting roles. That can be scary. As such, both parents need to be open to change and letting go of old routines. Experimenting with new approaches for a specified trial period can relieve some of the pressure and provide a safe space to try out and get used to new roles.

Financial Support

- My goal is to see that each of us—and our children—have enough income to meet our normal expenses, with a mechanism to take care of financial emergencies that might arise.
- One of my interests is to see that each of the children is assured a college education at a mutually-agreed-upon college.
- I have an interest in seeing my spouse pay spousal support until our youngest child is in school.

Tom and Mary also met with Barbara, their neutral financial advisor. With her support the parties gathered all their financial information. This data showed that Mary's income from her company is $200,000 per year, resulting in a net income of $13,500 per month. Tom had $5,000 per year in miscellaneous net income, or $416 per month.

Tom has a degree in social work, but he has not worked since their daughter was born. At that time, he felt strongly—and Mary agreed—

that he "be there" for the children for a period of time. Now Tom expresses a natural apprehension about reentering the workplace and discovers that he would need to take some classes in order to get recertified by the state.

The parties agreed conservatively that the entry-level salary for a social worker would be $25,000 annually. Barbara, the financial advisor, worked with both Tom and Mary to help them put together their individual estimated budgets for the next year, meaning that each of them came up with budgets that reflected the time each would spend with the children before Mary purchased her home and after the purchase was completed. The resulting "pre-house" budgets were $4,000 for Mary and $6,000 for Tom. On this basis, Tom and Mary agreed, subject to review by their Collaborative lawyers, that Mary would pay Tom child support of $2,100 per month and spousal maintenance of $6,000 per month. After Mary purchases her home and cares for the children half the time, the agreed-upon budgets will be $6,000 for Mary and $5,500 for Tom, and the support amounts would be adjusted accordingly ($1,500 child support and $6,000 spousal maintenance). The parties also agreed on a method of paying certain expenses for the children that are not related to where they are staying, such as school expenses, camps, lessons, and medical expenses not covered by insurance. It was agreed that they would each contribute $200 per month to a joint account to cover these specific expenses, the checkbook to travel back and forth with the children.

The recommendations only addressed the first year or so. How long the arrangement might last and when reductions might take place to adjust for Tom's expected return to the workplace would still need to be addressed by the parties with the support of their Collaborative lawyers. But Tom and Mary were off to a good start.

Support is usually divided into two main categories: child support (money paid to the caretaking parent for the purpose of caring for the children) and spousal support (money paid to support an ex-spouse). The divorce laws of the state involved usually include specific child-support guidelines that outline the amount of support to be paid, which is based on the number of children, the amount of time the children spend with each parent, and the parents' individual income levels. When one parent has sole custody of the children, the guideline amount sometimes is seen as mandatory. The more custody a parent has, the higher the child support award. In a sense, this creates an incentive for parents to seek more custody.

In Collaborative cases, the parties sometimes may ignore the rules laid down by the guidelines. They can focus instead on the needs of their children and themselves, and on how these needs can best be met. The parents often will set up a separate account (usually contributed to by both parties) to cover the cost of the children's activities.

Resolution of support issues is based on full disclosure of each parent's income and careful preparation, disclosure, and analysis of each one's estimated monthly living expenses for the immediate future. (See Appendix G for help with budget preparation.)

Property Issues

- I would like each of us to receive an equal portion of our marital assets.
- I would like to receive more retirement funds as part of my share, as I do not receive any retirement benefits from my employment.
- Because we would have to pay taxes on some of our assets if we sold them in the future, my interest is to take taxes into account in the asset division so we each receive assets calculated as if the taxes had been paid.

Marital property covers many different types of assets, including bank accounts, mutual funds, investment accounts, insurance (with cash value), IRAs, pensions, profit-sharing plans, 401(k), stocks, stock options, business interests, cars, boats, recreational vehicles, real estate holdings, time shares, and much more. All of these, and any other assets, need to be identified and valued. Here is where your Collaborative lawyer—and your neutral financial advisor if you have one—will be a big help.

The list of assets prepared by the professionals is like a menu, in that you and your spouse are able to pick and choose who gets what, and whether certain assets should be divided equally. We suggest that you go through this list carefully with your financial advisor so that all the tax implications can be factored properly into the prices. (The sample balance sheet on page 122 illustrates one way that this can work.)

John and Jane's Asset Balance Sheet

John and Jane have been married twenty-two years. Their children are fourteen and seventeen. John has been unhappy in the relationship for quite some time, and he has just decided that he wants out of the marriage. After an initial upset, Jane has agreed to a divorce and both have agreed to work Collaboratively to resolve their issues. They have also agreed to identify, value, and divide their marital assets equally, but, at this point, they are not concerned with the future income tax impact on specific assets.

As you can see from the balance sheet below, John and Jane have agreed that John will be keeping the house, subject to the mortgage on it. They are dividing some assets equally and others unequally to suit their preferences.

	Assets	John	Jane
House	$180,000	$180,000	
(Mortgage)	(77,088)	(77,088)	
Vehicles	20,000	10,000	10,000
Car Loan	(14,000)	(7,000)	(7,000)
Savings	7,000	3,500	3,500
Retirement	341,189	187,311	153,878
Wife's IRA	17,977	2,877	15,100
Husband's IRA	17,406	17,406	0
Investment Account	5,552	2,776	2,776
Art	184,086	52,586	131,500
Piano	5,700	5,700	0
Life Insurance	34,506	12,641	21,865
Silver Coin Collection	2,809	2,809	0
Miscellaneous Coin Collection	1,400	700	700
Business	13,000	13,000	0
Totals	**$739,537**	**$407,218**	**332,319**

Equal shares = $369,768.50 each

To equalize: John pays Jane $37,449.50 (*$407,218 minus $332,319*) divided by 2 = $37,449.50.

As part of the asset division, John is receiving $38,616 more than Jane in retirement funds on which taxes are due in the future. In this case, he was willing to consider these funds as equal to those funds without future liability without any adjustment.

Getting Clear on Asset Division

Often when meeting with clients early on, we'll hear things like, "We have the pension issue worked out. My wife says I can have it."

Clients often are relieved to share this good news, then sometimes puzzled that we're a little less certain of the issue's resolution than they are. As "lawyerly" as this may sound, in most cases what *sounds* like a final agreement between the spouses really isn't that simple.

When the wife told her husband that he could have his pension, was she expecting something of equal value or not? Maybe she was. Or maybe the thought of getting something in return hadn't yet crossed her mind. But, when all of the assets are added up, she'll have a chance to consider all aspects of the proposals carefully, with the help of her attorney as well. And, indeed, she may feel differently.

For example, let's assume that the pension is worth $200,000, and that the only other significant asset was their house, which was sold and netted the couple $200,000. Will they divide the house proceeds equally? If so, property division would look like this:

	Total value	Husband's share	Wife's share
House	$200,000	$100,000	$100,000
Pension	$200,000	$200,000	0
Total	$400,000	$300,000	$100,000

It's hard to believe that this was the property division the wife had in mind. If she'd had all of the information in front of her, she might have proposed that she take the profits from the house in exchange for the pension. In that case, the division would look more like this:

	Total value	Husband's share	Wife's share
House	$200,000	0	$200,000
Pension	$200,000	$200,000	0
Total	$400,000	$200,000	$200,000

That looks like a more equitable split, but is it? When the husband finds out that he may lose up to a third of his pension to taxes and the profits from the house were tax free, he may want to restructure things yet again. You see the pattern here.

In most cases, a couple's balance sheet has many more than two items on it. But the point is that until everyone has all the facts, no one can really be sure of what's on the table. It's also quite possible that a number of other issues, including parenting time and support, could affect the way assets are divided. That's why it's critical that you avoid jumping to early conclusions or finalizing arrangements before all the groundwork has been laid.

Now that you're familiar with some of the specific issues you may encounter, let's move on to a discussion of the steps you'll be taking to ensure a successful Collaborative process.

CHAPTER 7

Goals and Commitment:

The First Steps to Success in the Collaborative Process

Success via the Collaborative process comes down to determining what you really want (establishing your goals), determining what you are willing to do to achieve these goals (deciding what to commit to), and then deciding how to go about achieving your goals (crafting a strategy).

Setting and Prioritizing Goals and Interests

Do you know what you want—what you really want—out of this divorce? At this point you might be thinking, "I just want this divorce to be over," "I just want custody of my children," or "I just want to survive financially." While these are all good starting points, we encourage you to delve more deeply. Because some of the daily details of your divorce (such as how a particular bill will get paid this month) can have a greater sense of urgency than others, it is easy to fall into a pattern of putting all of your energy there. Remembering that big-picture concerns, such as the stability of your children and your long-term financial security, are really your most important goals will help you focus your time and resources on the issues that will have the greatest impact on your life in the years ahead.

Also, if you and your spouse each spend time identifying your big-picture goals at the outset, you will be likely to see that you share many common interests and concerns. Identifying shared goals will play an important role in helping you achieve your best possible outcome.

Thinking About What You Truly Want

Start by thinking about what truly matters to you, more than anything else, regardless of whether you think it relates to the divorce. You can then think about which of these broader goals or interests you want to achieve through the divorce process.

It's entirely possible that putting your marriage back together is one of your goals. This is understandable, even natural, particularly if you did not initiate the divorce. But for the purposes of figuring out what you want *from your divorce*, it's essential to assume that the divorce is going to happen. Focus on goals that relate to how you will live your life afterward.

What do you think will matter to you ten or twenty years from now? Thinking in these terms will help you separate your immediate, short-term goals (making sure your spouse pays the mortgage this month) from critical, long-term goals that seem too far in the future to wrap your head around (such as making sure your children continue to have a meaningful relationship with both parents).

Robert H. Mnookin, director of the Harvard Negotiation Research Project, a key exponent of innovative problem-solving techniques, reminds us in his book, *Beyond Winning* (The Belknap Press of Harvard University Press, Cambridge, MA, 2000), that your lawyer's goal is to focus on helping you understand your priorities and interests to enhance the problem-solving around the four-way table.

Knowing the Difference Between Interest and Positions

When we refer to *interests*, we're talking about basic needs that are related to your core goals in life. By contrast, a *position* is simply a way of stating what you want, regardless of whether or not it addresses a need. Take a look at the difference between what John *wants* and the *position* he's defending:

John's attorney: What is the main thing you want to achieve in your divorce?

John: I want joint physical custody of my children. That's what's most important to me.

John's attorney: Why do you want joint physical custody?

John: So that I can see my children at least half the time.

John's attorney: What if your wife agrees to a schedule that gives you exactly that, but won't agree to call the arrangement "joint physical custody"?

John: I guess that would be fine, as long as I get as much time as possible with my children.

In the example above, John's *interest* is having significant time with his children. Because he believed it was necessary to call it "joint custody," he automatically stated that *position* rather than think about how he might still get what he wants (maintain his interest, time with his children) regardless of the label.

John's situation is a common one, in which parents in the midst of a divorce often start by saying they want a particular type of custody (joint physical, sole physical, and so on) based on a limited understanding of what those labels actually mean. When asked why they feel so strongly about a particular label (position), parents generally identify their underlying interest (wanting a particular amount of time with the children, wanting a particular amount of support, wanting the children to remain in the state, and so on), which locks the other spouse into a position of pushing for a *different* custody label. As a result, emotions can flare and negotiations can stall un-

When Sue and Bob finally decided to end their twelve-year marriage, their main concern was the well-being of their two children, Daniel, age eight, and Emily, age three. During the marriage they'd both agreed that it would be better for the children if Sue stayed at home until Emily was in first grade. Now that they were getting divorced, it was unclear whether they were going to be able to afford for Sue to stay at home.

Determined to make this a priority, Sue went over her expenses with her sister and found a way to reduce her household expenses to $4,000 per month. However, she concluded there simply was no way to reduce her expenses below that point, and she felt she simply needed Bob to understand that $4,000 per month was her "bottom line." She discussed this position with her attorney.

Sue's attorney: Let's talk about what you want in terms of support.

Sue: I need $4,000 per month in family support. That's my bottom line.

Sue's attorney: Why do you believe you need $4,000 per month?

Sue: Because that would allow me to stay at home until Emily is in first grade. If Bob does not give me that amount, it will not be possible. We need to make that clear to him.

Sue's attorney: It sounds like your primary interest is in being able to stay home with Emily.

Sue: That's correct.

Sue's attorney: Bob's attorney is saying that Bob does want you to be able to stay home with Emily, but he cannot pay $4,000 per month and still meet his living expenses.

Sue: If Bob wants this to happen, he is simply going to have to find a way to pay the $4,000 per month.

Sue's attorney: What if he gave you $3,000 per month in family support and gave you an extra $24,000 from the mutual funds. You could draw an extra $1,000 per month from that account during the next two years until Emily is in school.

Sue: I guess that could work, as long as it allows me to stay home during these next two years.

necessarily. However, if the couple is allowed to explore their underlying interests without the verbiage of legal labels they rarely understand, there's a much greater chance of both getting what they want. They can then come up with a label they can both live with.

Differences between positions and interests also occur when parties are trying to reach agreements on financial issues. Consider the situation involving Sue and Bob:

This example, like the first one, is a much-simplified version of a very common scenario. Sue's position was that she needed $4,000 per month. However, her goal or interest was in being able to stay home with Emily. While Bob also had an interest in having Sue stay home with Emily for those two years, he could not agree with her position of needing $4,000 per month because that would mean he wouldn't have been able to meet his living expenses. Once they shifted away from positions, it was easier for the couple and their attorneys to identify ways in which they could achieve their common interest.

The interests versus positions dilemma is by no means limited to child custody and support-related issues. In looking at your financial situation, for example, you may have calculated a bottom-line dollar amount that you arrived at mathematically in a particular way (in this case, monthly payments). If your spouse uses the same approach and arrives at a different bottom line, you'll be stuck in different positions, feeling as if one of you will have to lose in order for the other to win. Shifting the discussion to focus on your interests, rather than your positions, helps to cultivate a greater understanding of what's important to each of you, and it increases the chances that both your needs will be met.

Other common positions we often hear from our clients:

- I want permanent spousal support.
- I want temporary spousal support.
- I want all of the tax exemptions.
- I want child support that equals the state guidelines.
- I want to have the children 50 percent of the time.
- I don't want to pay more than 50 percent of my income.
- I want my spouse to pay all of the debts.
- I want to keep my retirement account.
- I want my name off all of the debts.

So what makes these statements positions instead of interests?

- It's not immediately clear *why* you want what you say you want. (What's only clear is that you *think* you want it.)
- These statements do not necessarily relate to core needs or values.
- It's not clear that the client truly understands what some of the terms mean.
- It is possible that the client could obtain something of equal value through another method.
- Each of these statements tends to create a win-lose scenario in that only one person ends up with the thing that he or she identified.

To put you in a goal-and-interest mind-set, we have provided many more examples of common goals and interests in Appendix E.

Prioritizing Your Goals

It's pretty unlikely that you'll be able to achieve every single one of your goals, so it's essential to try for the ones most important to you first. Prioritizing will help you make decisions when it is time to make compromises in the process. The hope is that you both can compromise a less-important goal in order to achieve a more-important one, reaching resolution.

There are many ways that you can choose to prioritize your goals:

- List your goals in order of importance.
- Review your list and determine which interests can easily be eliminated. Then make a second list of interests you could give up if you had to (knowing you'd rather have them).
- Continually update and refine your list by asking yourself the following questions:

  - Are my goals realistic?
  - Is this goal/interest so important to me that I would be willing to make a major sacrifice in order to be able to achieve it?
  - Is this a goal that can be achieved during the divorce process?
  - Would I regard this goal as legitimate if my spouse had the same goal?
  - Is this really an interest or is it a position?
  - Will this goal really matter to me ten years from now? Twenty years from now?

- Is this goal based partly on spite?
- Is this goal consistent with my values?
- Is this goal really as important as the other goals?
- Would my spouse have to make an unreasonable sacrifice in order for me to achieve this goal?

By defining and prioritizing your goals and interests, you've taken a major step toward achieving a successful resolution of your divorce issues. Once you put your list together, keep a written copy in a place where you can refer to it regularly.

Now let's see how committed you are to making your goals a reality.

Making the Commitment Necessary to Achieving Success

As we've seen in working with our numerous clients, and as we've said throughout this book, the outcome of your case really does depend on you. The biggest indicator of success is the level of commitment that both you and your spouse are willing to make emotionally, financially, and in terms of time:

Emotional commitment: Your willingness to endure discomfort or emotional hardship in order to achieve your goals.

Time commitment: Your willingness to commit the time necessary to achieve your goals.

Financial commitment: Your willingness to commit the financial resources necessary to achieve your goals.

Let's look at each of these commitments more closely.

The Emotional Commitment

The Collaborative process, with its emphasis on four-way meetings and direct communication, requires a significant emotional commitment from both you and your spouse. What we're talking about is the discomfort you may feel at having to work directly with your spouse on issues of great importance to both of you during a very difficult time. While direct communication sometimes presents emotional challenges, in most Collaborative cases it's a necessary ingredient for success—especially when children are involved. Ultimately, you may need to tolerate a certain level of discomfort in order to achieve the best outcome. But if the situation becomes too uncomfortable, there are ways in which you can address your feelings of discomfort. You can, for example, take as many breaks as necessary during the four-way meetings. You can use these breaks either to collect yourself by going for a walk or phoning a friend, or you can use this time to talk to your attorney or coach about ways to make the meeting more comfortable for you. In some instances, you can choose to suspend the direct four-way meetings and conduct the meetings through smaller "sub-caucuses," in which you meet with your attorney (or both attorneys) in one room, and the attorneys meet with your spouse in a separate room. While sub-caucusing generally is less effective than the full four-way meeting, you should discuss this option with your attorney if you are unable to make the four-way meetings work for you. It's certainly a better alternative than giving up and going to court.

Getting Help

Divorce coaches can help you prepare for the emotional challenge of the four-way meetings.

Some clients are reluctant to hire coaches, believing that working with a mental-health professional in this capacity is acknowledging some significant shortcoming. Be reassured: You do not have to suffer from any psychological or emotional abnormality to benefit from coaching, nor does the fact that you do benefit from coaching indicate a psychological problem! It may help to know that even the healthiest, best adjusted among us generally lack the skills to address the emotional upheavals of divorce effectively. Coaching provides an opportunity to bolster these emotional resources, and it provides you with a safe, reliable support system.

The Time Commitment

If you're going to achieve your goals, you're likely going to need to make a substantial investment of time. Sometimes you'll spend that time doing something that needs to be done to further the divorce process, such as preparing for and attending meetings or gathering information. Other times, you'll spend your time waiting or thinking, which can feel like everything from healing to frustrating.

When we talk to our clients about the time commitment a divorce takes, many underestimate it. "How long could it take?" we often hear. But once the process is underway, most are surprised by how long the process can last. While a divorce utilizing the Collaborative process generally takes less time than a traditional divorce, you need to be prepared for the fact that the divorce may take longer than you want it to. In our experience, the average divorce using the traditional process takes between eight and fourteen months to complete, while the average Collaborative divorce takes between four and eight months. However, many divorces using either of these processes can go well beyond these parameters. The main difference is that, while a litigated divorce sometimes can take several years if things spiral out of control, a Collaborative divorce generally does not stretch out over a long period of time unless you and your spouse choose to move more slowly. There are many clients who choose to move at a deliberate pace in a Collaborative process, or to put the divorce on hold while they are working on reconciliation or waiting for other events to occur.

While slowing down your divorce is relatively easy, if both spouses agree, speeding up your divorce can more difficult. Getting a divorce doesn't eliminate any of your other responsibilities. Most

Brad did not think his divorce from Stephanie would be very complicated. Although they had been married for fifteen years and had three small children, they had already worked out their custody and child-support issues before they met with the attorneys, and they knew they wanted to divide their property equally. The only issue they had not finalized, in Brad's view, was alimony, but he didn't anticipate any trouble because he had already agreed to pay alimony for three years so that Stephanie could continue to work part time until their youngest child was in school.

Brad had moved out of the house two months before they started the divorce and was living with his brother in a suburb thirty miles from their home. He was eager to have a house of his own and to live closer to the children. Prior to the first four-way meeting he put $10,000 down on a house with the expectation that their negotiation would be done within sixty days so that he could close on the house and move in.

Unfortunately the alimony issue became more difficult than Brad had imagined. From the beginning, Brad had determined that the most he could pay in alimony was $1,500 per month. However, during their second meeting, he learned that Stephanie's budget showed she needed at least $2,200 per month in addition to the $2,000 in child support that he had already agreed to pay. Brad could not see how

Stephanie could need that much cash to meet her budget! Moreover, he couldn't imagine that anyone seriously could expect him to pay that amount. Brad's attorney had encouraged him to put together a detailed budget of his own and to carefully review Stephanie's budget, as well as some prior bank records, so that everyone had all of the facts before them while they were reviewing this critical question. However, this was the busy season in Brad's business and he wasn't able to get these tasks completed before the first two meetings. In addition, the attorneys had suggested that Brad work with a financial neutral to help work through these budget issues. But Brad didn't want to incur the expense of hiring another expert, and he feared that bringing in another professional would lead to more delay and unnecessary expense.

After making little progress on this issue after three meetings, Brad reluctantly agreed to take some more time to review the budgets and meet with the financial neutral and his attorney to help crunch the numbers. In the course of these meetings, he discovered that there was a way to restructure his payments in a way that he would save approximately $300 per month in taxes. At the fifth meeting, Brad and Stephanie finally reached an agreement on alimony and signed a full Marital Termination Agreement. Unfortunately, because of the financial uncertainty of the prior several months, Brad was forced to cancel his purchase agreement on the house and had to forfeit his earnest money.

In the end, the divorce took approximately ten months, much longer than Brad had anticipated. Looking back Brad realized that, had he done a better job managing his expectations about time and had set aside more time to work with his attorney and financial neutral earlier in the process, he would have saved himself thousands of dollars and much frustration.

people are already busy with their jobs, their family lives, and social and civic duties. Making room for a divorce is tougher than it sounds, even if it is a priority. Trying to rush through the divorce can lead you to make quick decisions without fully considering all of your options.

If you don't set aside enough time, and instead try to shoehorn your divorce into an already busy life, you'll be adding to your already-high stress levels and reducing your ability to function well at a time when you need to be as rested, thoughtful, and clear-headed as possible.

So start thinking now about canceling (at least for a while) some discretionary activities to leave room for the divorce. But *don't* cut back on activities that help you sustain your morale or mental health. If going fishing or spending an evening hanging out with your best friend gives you the strength to do what you need to do, do it—and enjoy.

The Financial Commitment

Divorce often comes at a time of financial strain, and it's natural for separating couples to be very anxious about how much the divorce will cost them. In fact, a lot of people start exploring the Collaborative option because they see it as a way to reduce expenses.

But while it's true that the Collaborative process generally is far less expensive than litigation, achieving the outcome you want still may cost more than you'd hope to pay in an ideal world. That's why it's important to prepare yourself for the financial cost of divorce as much as possible.

Determining What a Divorce Should Cost or
How Much You Should Be Prepared to Spend

If you've talked with people who have been through a divorce, you probably know that there's no such thing as a "typical" cost.

And if you ask, most attorneys will refuse to give you an estimate or will come back with one of the legal profession's favorite phrases, "It depends." As annoying as that may be to hear, in truth, the cost *does* depend on a number of different factors that are nearly impossible to predict with any degree of accuracy.

That said, there are some ways to at least ballpark what the di-

Bob and Diane were hoping that using the Collaborative process would help them keep their costs down. However, they knew there would be some important issues to make decisions on. They had been married for twenty-eight years and had three children, Brian, who was now twenty and a sophomore in college; Dean, who had just turned eighteen and would graduate from high school this year; and Mary, who was thirteen and just entering the eighth grade. Diane was an engineer who was earning approximately $120,000 per year and had provided the primary support for the family. Bob had suspended his medical technician career to stay home with the children for ten years and was now working part-time, earning $28,000 per year.

Even though they were both committed to finding a solution, they were not sure how they were going to make the numbers add up, and their attorneys both advised them to prepare for the fact that it would take some work to find an acceptable solution.

They had approximately $23,000 in a mutual-fund account that they decided to set aside to cover legal fees, expert expenses, and fees charged by other team members. They agreed that they would split anything left over and use the proceeds to reward themselves.

The divorce took approximately seven months, but they were able to complete everything for approximately $17,000, mostly because they both learned to let go of minor issues that were holding them back. For example, Diane thought that Bob was getting most of the personal household goods and wanted to receive an extra $4,000 from their savings to offset the difference. Bob did not agree that he was getting more of the household goods and believed that Diane had received at least half of the value. Their attorneys informed them that they could get an appraisal of the household goods. However, neither one of them wanted to pay the estimated $3,000 that an appraiser would charge, plus the additional attorneys' fees that they might incur in working to resolve the issue once the appraisal was finished. Diane eventually agreed that the difference was not worth incurring the extra expense and decided to let it go.

In addition, Bob thought that he should get an extra $1,800 from the savings to offset the $1,800 that Diane had taken from the mutual fund to pay for a trip with her sister just before the separation. Diane disagreed, since she maintained that Bob had spent a similar amount from the savings account to make some home improvements eight months earlier. While Bob initially thought he should stick to this issue because of the "principle," he ultimately realized that it just did not make sense to continue to dispute that amount.

After they both let go of these final issues and settled the case, they divided up the remaining $6,000. Bob used his share to take a winter golf trip with some of his college friends. Diane used hers to purchase a new stereo system for her entertainment center.

vorce will cost you. We'll talk about several of them in the following pages, and, as you're doing your estimates, make sure to consider the *total* costs—that's your attorneys' legal fees *plus* filing fees, expert fees, and fees charged by other professionals on your team.

Once your attorney is familiar with the issues in your case, he or she can give you a general estimate about the types of fees and expenses that you might anticipate in your case. Ask your attorney to help you make a more conservative high estimate so that you can be prepared to address almost any scenario.

The Advantages of a High Estimate

Because it's so hard to predict the total cost of a divorce accurately, we suggest that you estimate a much higher amount than you think you'll actually need. This has several advantages:

- Setting aside adequate funds will allow you to hire the professionals you need to get the best possible outcome for your situation.
- Underestimating costs could leave you without the ability to access the necessary funds when you need them the most.
- If you set aside more than you will need, you can afford a little reward for coming in under budget. You could take a vacation, buy a nice gift, or redecorate a room in your new house.

Jolene and Mark believed that they would not have much difficulty working out the issues in their divorce. They had been married sixteen years and had one child, Tom, who had just turned six. While their attorneys cautioned them to prepare for the fact that there could be some expense in determining the nonmarital interests in their house and stock because of a significant inheritance that Jolene had received during the marriage, Mark had been hoping that his legal fees would be less than $3,000. But when $3,000 came and went and the case still wasn't settled, he became anxious and frustrated. He was so concerned about not racking up any more fees that he ultimately made some concessions just to get the divorce over with. Those concessions cost him at least $10,000 more than he would have spent to see the divorce through properly.

- Finishing the process under budget will also give you the intangible reward of ending the divorce on a high note.

In most Collaborative cases, the total costs for both attorneys, coaches, expert fees, filing fees, and so on will be less than what you'd spend to sell your house (around 6 to 8 percent in commissions, closing costs, and so on). As a rule of thumb, setting aside 5 percent of the value of your house most likely will cover your Collaborative divorce costs.

Evaluating Legal Services

Because lawyers charge on an hourly basis, it's tempting to try to assess whether you're getting your money's worth for each hour of the lawyer's time. But that's not a particularly effective way to deter-

---

Over the course of nine months, Joan's divorce lawyer spent fifty hours on her traditional divorce. At $200 per hour, Joan's legal fees came to $10,000. The billable time charged by Joan's lawyer involved the following tasks:

- Listened to Joan describe her circumstances and concerns
- Advised her on the law
- Helped Joan understand and evaluate her options
- Received information from the other attorney
- Communicated with the other attorney through letters and phone calls
- Drafted motion papers for court
- Talked to potential witnesses
- Drafted and revised documents
- Gathered information
- Reviewed and analyzed documents

- Made written and oral arguments on Joan's behalf to the other attorney
- Made arguments on her behalf to the court
- Conducted formal discovery
- Drafted other formal papers for the court: motions, affidavits, and so on.

Looking back on her case, Joan tried to figure out whether everything the lawyer did on her behalf was worth $200 per hour. Some blocks of time—like the hour Joan and her lawyer waited around in the courtroom hallway—weren't even worth $10 an hour! Some of the arguments the attorney made on her behalf probably were worth $400 an hour, since it felt great to have someone sticking up for her. But those same arguments ended up infuriating her husband and made it much more difficult to settle the case, so that time may have actually cost Joan more than it saved.

The hour the attorney spent advising Joan about the settlement turned out to have been extremely valuable, because it generated a tax savings idea that will save Joan thousands of dollars over the coming years. She estimated that that hour may have been worth at least $1,000 dollars.

mine what something should cost, especially in a divorce case, where it's not always clear what you're hiring your lawyer to do. Consider the following scenario:

As you can see, it's very hard to determine the value of legal services in the traditional process, particularly when you break the services down by the hour. In Collaborative cases, sometimes it can be even more difficult. Since Collaborative lawyers don't engage in arguments, you won't be billed for time spent arguing with the other side. It may be just as well, since most arguments turn out to be counterproductive (and overly expensive) anyway.

Odd as it may seem, the very best Collaborative legal work is practically invisible. Perhaps one of the most valuable things that your Collaborative lawyer will do for you is create an atmosphere in which settlement is possible. If this happens, and you end up with an agreement that allows you to parent your children effectively, for example, those atmosphere-creation skills are priceless. If your four-way meetings went smoothly and you reached a settlement easily, you may have barely noticed your lawyer doing much of anything.

How to Be an Effective Consumer of Legal (and Other Services)

Divorce, even under the best of circumstances, usually isn't cheap. So we encourage you to think about what you're purchasing, just as you would with any other major expenditure. As you go through each task that needs to be completed in your divorce, think about whether you really need professional help. In a lot of cases you'll find that you can handle the job yourself. For example, you'll need to gather certain information about your income and assets. Most people can do some, if not all, of that information-gathering on their own.

In other cases, you may have some of the necessary skills but could use some help from an expert. For example, you probably can put together a pretty good estimated budget yourself. But paying for an hour or two with a CPA or other professional could save you money in the long run by helping you better anticipate your needs.

In still other areas, you'll have to rely entirely on other people to get the job done. For example, assessing the value of a business or determining the tax implications of your settlement are tasks best left to the professionals.

Part of being an effective consumer is honestly deciding what you can do on your own, what you need some assistance with, and what you need to turn over entirely to an expert.

Think in terms of building a house. If you've got the skills and the time and inclination to use them, you can save yourself a lot of money by doing certain things yourself. But it's up to you to figure out where to draw the line, how much your time is worth, and whether, in the interests of getting the job done and done right, you might want to let someone else handle certain things. The best house, as with the best divorce, is not always the cheapest one. And the house that's best for you isn't necessarily the same house that's best for your neighbor.

Now that you've identified your goals and determined your level of commitment to the Collaborative process, it's time to start putting together strategies to help you achieve the best possible outcome for your situation. Part Four takes you through each stage of the Collaborative process and helps you develop those strategies.

PART FOUR

A Step-by-Step Guide Through
the Collaborative Process

Because the first four-way meeting is significantly different from any of those that follow, we've devoted chapter 8 to preparing for four-way meetings in general, and chapter 9 to what actually happens in the first meeting. In chapter 10, we'll cover subsequent meetings, as well as some of the specific events that may unfold as the process continues.

Although we're emphasizing meetings, what happens in the time between the four-ways can be almost as important as what happens during the meetings. In chapter 11, we'll go over the homework you're going to need to do to get the most out of your meetings, and what happens next in those rare situations when the Collaborative process breaks down.

In chapter 12, we move beyond meetings and address finalizing your divorce, detailing what it takes to make that happen. Finally, in chapter 13, we reflect on what it means to put the divorce behind you and focus on the days ahead.

CHAPTER 8

Preparing for the Four-Way Meetings

A t this stage in the process, we are assuming that you and your spouse each have retained a Collaborative lawyer. If you haven't, please reread chapter 3. This chapter outlines the steps necessary to prepare for the all-important first four-way meeting.

Information Gathering

The very first step after retaining your lawyers is to gather all the financial information that is relevant to your case. If you have retained a neutral financial expert to assist you (see chapter 4), he or she probably will give each of you a detailed list of exactly what you need. In case you're not working with a financial expert, we've provided a list of the documents you and your spouse will most likely be asked to collect:

- Income tax returns for the past three years
- Most recent W-2 forms for each party for each employment during the year
- Most recent pay stubs for the most recent month

- Most recent statements for 401(k)s, employee pensions, IRAs, Roth IRAs, and other retirement accounts
- Most recent statement for each joint and individual non-retirement investment account. This should include an itemized list of all stocks, bonds, CDs, and so on.
- Copies of all outstanding stock options
- Copies of all life insurance statements, including cash value balances
- Legal description of all real estate holdings
- Most recent mortgage statements for all real property owned, either individually or jointly, indicating balance and payment amount
- Complete list of all of your joint and individual debts
- Preliminary list of monthly expenses (for a sample monthly budget, see Appendix G)
- Most recent bank statements, both individual and joint
- List of cars and recreational vehicles and a statement of how much (if anything) you owe
- List of businesses owned and current balance sheet for each

Meeting with Your Attorney

One or two weeks before the first four-way meeting, you and your attorney should get together to go over what the four-way process is about, what it looks like, how it works, and the role each person plays.

Your attorney probably will have a checklist of specific topics to cover. But just so you're prepared, read through the list below. If any of the items in the list aren't covered by your attorney, feel free to bring them up.

What About Assets Owned Prior to the Marriage, or What About My Inheritance?

Both parties will need to sort out their issues concerning property owned individually before they were married. Again, you need to check with your Collaborative lawyer in your location, as the laws vary. In many states, if the previously owned property or cash is still around, either in its original form or traceable to another asset, the initial owner usually gets to keep it without sharing with the other spouse—including any appreciation in value. If income from such assets has been reinvested, that income is not considered nonmarital and is devisable. The same rule often applies to gifts or inheritances received by one party either before or during the marriage, if it is still identifiable and not thoroughly intermixed with marital funds. Complications arise where the nonmarital funds have been invested in the marital home and marital funds have been used for mortgage reduction and improvements. Experts are available to help sort out such nonmarital claims. Remember, just because the law may give you certain rights regarding nonmarital claims, that does not mean you have to exercise those rights at all or in the same way the court might. Keep your options open to look at the big picture.

- An agreement on the time and place of the first meeting: Normally the four-ways will alternate between the two attorneys' offices. But if one office is more conveniently located, you can decide to have most or all of your meetings there. The location has no bearing on who's got the upper hand in the negotiation. Keep in mind that attorneys typically charge door-to-door, so try to find a meeting place that minimizes the amount of time the lawyers will have to travel.

- The agenda for the first four-way meeting: Because the first meeting deals mostly with procedures and ground rules, the agenda most likely will have been prepared by the attorneys. (The general practice is that the lawyers are in charge of procedure and the clients are in charge of substantive matters.) Agendas for future meetings, however, will include you and your spouse's input. A typical agenda for the first four-way meeting might look something like this:

- Discuss why you and your spouse have chosen Collaborative law and your key hopes for the process.
- Review, discuss, and sign the Participation Agreement, which, as you may remember, states that the lawyers will withdraw from the case if it turns adversarial. See Appendix A for an example of an actual Participation Agreement.
- Review, discuss, and sign ground rules.
- Review and sign Joint Petition (or Petition—this is the document that officially starts the divorce).
- Review the marital issues that need to be resolved.
- Set two or three times and places for subsequent meetings.
- Assign homework.

- All four participants agree to communicate naturally, respectfully, and in a way that facilitates settlement.
- Approach the conference with a spirit of goodwill. Just keeping this in mind often has the effect of making the meeting room much more conducive to settlement.
- Communication in the four-way meeting can go in any direction. You can talk to your spouse's lawyer, your lawyer, or your spouse, and each of them can talk to you and each other. (See "Good Communication" on page 154 for more information.)
- Your lawyer should advise you that he or she will be paying

special attention to your spouse during the four-way in order to help establish a trusting, non-adversarial relationship. Your spouse's attorney probably will be doing the same with you.

- Your spouse's attorney is part of the team put in place to help with settlement, as is your spouse. (See "Your Relationship with Your Spouse's Attorney, below.") That's why, if at all possible, it's beneficial for the couple to choose their lawyers together. Don't be alarmed by your spouse's lawyer's interest in you, or your attorney's interest in your spouse.

- One of the attorneys will take and prepare minutes of the meeting. This role may alternate.

- In general, the meeting should last no more than two hours. Our experience has shown that participants lose their mental edge if the sessions go much longer. (The words *testy* and *foggy* come to mind!)

- Most discussions will be conducted with all four persons in the room at the same time. However, you can take a break and meet one on one with your lawyer (caucus) at any time.

- When at all possible, you and your spouse will be expected to take the initiative in discussing issues and needs, but it is fair to expect the attorneys to guide you through the agenda.

Your Relationship with Your Spouse's Attorney

In a traditional divorce your relationship with your spouse's attorney is an adversarial one, and the assumption is that he or she is plotting to do you in. In Collaboration the relationships between the spouses and their attorneys are very different.

Around the four-way table you'll probably begin to see your spouse's attorney as part of the settlement team, and you may speak freely with him or her. In some instances you might begin to feel

Good Communication

Good communication is a critical part of the Collaborative process. It starts with the understanding that during the four-way meeting, any of the participants can speak directly to any of the others. For example, you can talk with your spouse and/or your spouse's attorney, and vice versa.

Keep the conversational tone respectful, and focus on the future. This is not the time for blame or accusations or rehashing anything negative that may have happened during the marriage. Anger and emotional outbursts, while not uncommon, waste settlement time and rack up attorney fees. If you or your spouse are having difficulty staying focused during your four-way meetings, consider adding a divorce coach to your settlement team to help you learn to communicate more clearly.

One of the hardest—and most important—parts of communication is listening. Rather than rehearsing your next zinger while someone else is talking, open your ears—and your mind. You may find it helpful to repeat back what you hear, just to make sure you understood ("So what I heard you say was . . . is that correct?") If you didn't get it right, ask for a repeat. Check out the ground rules in Appendix H for more tips on improving communication.

that you like your spouse's lawyer better than your own! There is nothing wrong or incorrect about this impression. In fact, it can often enhance the settlement mode—particularly if your spouse is developing a similar relationship with your attorney. However, remember that your attorney is representing you and your spouse's attorney is representing your spouse's interests. In order to maintain the integrity of the process, there are limits to how you should relate to your spouse's attorney.

For example, in the four-way you could ask the other attorney a legal question—but you should not call him or her outside the session and ask that same question.

Interest-Based Negotiations

The Collaborative divorce process is a client-centered process, which means that the lawyers will not get involved in fighting over positions. Instead, we do everything we can to keep settlement conversations moving forward.

To do that, we utilize—and teach our clients—a relatively new and unique way to negotiate called *interest-based negotiation*. Interest-based negotiations distinguish clearly between interests and positions. (For example, "I want the house!" is a position, while "We need to provide a familiar stable ongoing environment for the children" is an interest.) When you and your spouse are able to keep your eyes on your interests, there usually are ways to negotiate a win-win resolution in which both of you can get what you want (or at least close to it).

Brainstorming

Another useful tool in four-way work is suggesting that everyone around the table throw out ideas (without criticism or judgment) as options for handling a particular issue that seems difficult to resolve. If either lawyer proposes something, it should be clear to everyone that it's a *suggestion* and it has not necessarily been agreed to by the client.

Your Attorney's Role in the Four-Way Conference

In a litigation setting, your lawyer is your mouthpiece. He or she will defend and support whatever you're asking for and whatever positions you might hold on issues—reasonable or unreasonable. Your litigation lawyer may literally and figuratively pound the table and, if necessary to advance your position, belittle your spouse and the other attorney in the process.

Collaborative lawyers must often restrain themselves from strongly supporting positions expressed by a client in a four-way conference. You're perfectly free to express any position you like, but if it's too far out of the range of what's reasonable, having a lawyer jump in to support you can jeopardize the settlement climate. It can also result in the attorney losing credibility at a crucial point in the settlement process.

At the same time, if you didn't get any verbal support from your attorney when you expressed your position, you might feel that he or she isn't doing a good enough job acting as your advocate. That can lead you and your attorney to feel at odds with each other. In some instances, your attorney will be able to explain on the spot why your position won't work. Bottom line: Before raising any potentially sticky issue in a four-way meeting, run it by your attorney.

Reviewing the Participation Agreement

This is the document that controls how Collaboration works. Your lawyer should give you a copy for your review prior to the first four-way meeting. You and your spouse will review this agreement at the first meeting and, after everyone agrees to its conditions, both of you and your lawyers will sign it.

The exact wording of the Participation Agreement may vary from state to state or attorney to attorney, but the example in Appendix A is fairly typical.

The purpose of this document is to get all four participants on the same page and committed to the same principles. A fair amount of time is often spent at the first four-way meeting discussing these commitments and the philosophy of Collaboration.

Ground Rules

These are the general guidelines for communication during the four-way conferences and at any other point during the divorce process. Each Collaborative law region has its own version. The ground rules in Appendix H are from Minnesota, but they're fairly representative of the kinds of rules that would be covered almost anywhere.

The information has now been gathered to the best of your abilities. You've met with your attorney, the time and place for the meeting has been set, and a tentative agenda has been proposed. You are ready for your first four-way meeting.

CHAPTER 9

The First Collaborative
Four-Way Meeting

While all of your four-way meetings are important, the first one has particular significance because it usually sets the tone for those that follow. If you get off to a good start at the first meeting, the goodwill and momentum you create generally will exist throughout the rest of the process. Your attorney can help you set realistic and measurable expectations for the first four-way. If your expectations aren't consistent with the agenda for the first meeting, your attorney can help you either adjust your expectations or modify the agenda.

What May Happen at the First Meeting

While it's impossible for anyone to predict exactly how your first meeting will go, here's what happens in a typical first meeting:

- **You will meet your spouse's attorney for the first time and begin to establish a rapport.** Even though your attorney will have prepped you about how your spouse's attorney isn't going to be adversarial, sometimes it's hard to avoid coming into a first meeting with a negative view of the other side. After all, you've probably seen dozens of movies or TV shows where the attorneys were hostile, and you might have heard about similar real-life situations from friends or family. One of the goals of this first four-way meeting is to eliminate some of the preconceived notions you may have about your spouse's attorney so you can form a good working relationship.

Your spouse's attorney will be very interested in getting to know you and in establishing rapport with you as well. Even though he or she was hired as your spouse's advocate, it's understood that your spouse won't be able to achieve his or her goals unless your interests are protected as well.

- **Your attorney will establish a rapport with your spouse.** Chances are good that your spouse and your attorney are meeting for the first time. You'll need to understand that your lawyer will be bending over backward to establish rapport and to even demonstrate empathy with your spouse. This may seem odd at first, but keep in mind that it's really in your interest.

- **You will review and sign the Participation Agreement.** Your Collaborative divorce hasn't truly started until the Participation Agreement is signed. At this point you will have already reviewed it, but the lawyers will want to go through it in detail to make sure that everyone understands its terms. This is your best opportunity to ask questions and to deepen your commitment to the Collaborative process.

The amount of time you spend reviewing the Participation Agreement and the method used for the review may vary based on the standards established in the community where you live. In some areas, Collaborative attorneys prefer to spend more than an hour reviewing the Participation Agreement. In many other areas it takes as little as ten to thirty minutes. In some parts of the country, the parties and the attorneys take turns reading the document out loud. In other places, the attorneys simply summarize the document and encourage you and your spouse to ask questions. While you may feel this is a waste of precious time and money, think of it as a ceremonial laying of the ground rules. In truth, the attorneys spend as much time as they do going over the Participation Agreement so that no one can claim later they weren't clear on what they were committing to.

After the Participation Agreement is signed, each party generally is given a copy (or a duplicate original) of the document and you are ready to move on to the next step of the process.

• **You may sign a Joint Petition.** In an adversarial divorce, one spouse serves the Petition on the other. In the Collaborative process, you and your spouse most likely will use a Joint Petition (if that's allowed under the laws of your state or country), so that neither of you has to be served. Your attorney will tell you how this document is handled in your area and will explain its significance.

• **You and your spouse may talk about why you have chosen the Collaborative process.** While the Participation Agreement may cover many reasons why you might pursue this option, in general it is helpful for you and your spouse to be able to say, in your own words, why you are doing it this way. Beyond specific interests that will have value to each of you, this statement of intent and commitment to the Collaborative process has a way of shedding light on what really matters overall to the divorcing couple: divorcing with dignity and preserving the integrity of the relationship after the divorce.

- **You and your spouse will talk about your goals and interests.** The initial four-way meeting might be the first opportunity you and your spouse will have to talk with each other about your goals and your interests. In a lot of cases, you'll find that the two of you share many of them. Hopefully this will help you remember that your spouse doesn't have to lose in order for you to win—and vice versa.

- **You will identify the issues that need to be resolved.** You and your spouse, with the help of your attorneys, will lay out the major issues in your case. For a general list of the issues that can come up in a divorce case, see Appendix B (simply ignore the ones that don't apply in your situation).

  If you and your spouse have already resolved some issues, this is a good time to go over the agreements so they can be noted in the minutes. Be prepared, however, as touched upon previously, to renegotiate these agreements, since they may have been made without both you and your spouse having access to all the information you needed.

- **You will exchange and review documents.** This is a good time to identify the documents and explain anything that isn't completely obvious. For example, there may be a number of deductions from your paycheck that aren't going to be clear to either of the attorneys. Or, if you are self-employed, you might need to explain some terms or practices that are specific to your industry.

- **You may gather information by asking and answering questions.** Be prepared for your spouse's attorney to ask you questions. In the traditional method, attorneys generally are discouraged from asking questions of the other party unless it's part of a formal procedure in which you are under oath and a court reporter is recording your answers. During those formal procedures, your attorney would caution you to be very careful how you answer, because the opposing attorney might be trying to lure you into giving answers that could later be used against you.

In the Collaborative process, your answers cannot and will not be used against you. All information you provide is confidential unless you eventually agree, in writing, otherwise. In addition, your spouse's attorney will not try to entrap you because he or she knows that doing so would endanger the safe and effective environment that is crucial to the process. In order to make sure the information that you provide is truthful, your spouse or your spouse's attorney can ask for documentation or other corroboration. In addition, as part of the settlement process, you both will sign a statement, under oath, stating that you have fully and accurately disclosed all relevant facts. This gives you all of the safeguards of the traditional process without the wasteful and paralyzing procedures that often accompany formal methods of discovery.

Your attorney will likely encourage you to answer the questions in the same manner as if you were explaining your situation to a friend. This commitment to candor and transparency will be reciprocated by your spouse and will allow important information to come out in much less time than it would take during the traditional process.

You may decide to ask direct questions of your spouse. (If you choose to do so, make sure you do it in a way that doesn't come across as accusatory or inflammatory. Also, take a look at Appendix H.)

Similarly, your spouse will be able to ask you questions. If you feel uncomfortable answering a question for any reason, say so.

The attorneys will listen to your concerns and will offer some suggestions as to how the information can be exchanged in a more productive manner.

• **You will identify and discuss additional information that may be needed.** No matter how much you prepare for the first four-way meeting, there's always some piece of information that you didn't realize would be needed. Your attorneys will help you and your spouse identify exactly what's required and when it needs to be presented. (For more on homework, see chapter 11.)

• **You may discuss the possible need for experts.** Most cases require some help from experts, such as appraisers, realtors, pension evaluators, business evaluators, tax experts, and so on (for more on this, see chapter 4). If you and your spouse determine that expert help is needed, your attorneys will help you locate the appropriate people and bring them on board.

• **You will discuss adding other team members.** As covered in chapter 4, having other people on your team can be a big help. Now's a good time to figure out whether you and your spouse could benefit from bringing in coaches, financial neutrals, or child specialists. This may also be a time to consider whether you'd like to have a mediator available to help resolve potentially difficult issues. While mediation has been described in this book as a separate process, there are times in which the Collaborative process and mediation can be used together. Skilled mediators, because they are neutrals, can bring a new perspective to a particular problem and can, in the right circumstances, allow you to get the best of both worlds.

• **You may resolve some temporary issues.** It is unlikely that you'll have enough time in the first meeting to reach any significant agreements. Nevertheless, there may be some issues that will need to be taken care of long before your next four-way. For example, if there are bills that need to be paid imminently and you and your spouse can't agree on how to pay them, you should bring this up at the first four-way meeting. Of course if children are involved, you'll want to work out temporary solutions so that the kids won't be caught in the middle.

It's important to make clear that agreements on immediate concerns are simply Band-Aids, designed to stop the bleeding immediately until the issue can be addressed properly. These Band-Aid solutions can be adjusted at any time, and they should not be considered in any way permanent or something that sets a precedent for how things will be handled in the future.

• **You may determine ground rules for safe and effective two-way meetings between you and your spouse.** If you and your spouse intend to work on some issues in between four-way meetings, be sure to discuss the ground rules for those meetings. As desirable as it is to have you and your spouse work out issues on your own, take care to provide the right environment so that these meetings don't cause more problems than they solve. (See "Safe and Effective Environments" on page 105.)

• **You will have homework that needs to be done before the next meeting.** During the first four-way meeting, a number of tasks will be identified that need to be taken care of before the next meeting. We discuss homework in greater detail in chapter 11.

• **You will schedule the next meeting or meetings.** Be sure to bring your calendar to the first meeting. In determining when to schedule the next meeting, make sure that you leave yourself enough time to complete the homework, engage outside experts, and make the emotional adjustments.

While there may be situations in which scheduling the next meeting is deferred, your attorneys will urge you to schedule at least one, tentatively, with the understanding that it can always be moved if you and/or your spouse aren't ready to proceed. The attorneys have the responsibility to manage the process and may be concerned that leaving the meeting date open could damage some of the necessary structure that is needed to provide confidence in the process.

Jim and Sally were seeking divorce after ten years of marriage. They did not have children but had property and alimony issues that needed to be resolved. Jim, a surgeon, had experienced severe stress during the last three years of the marriage and had to take a leave of absence from his employment. In describing his circumstances during the second four-way meeting, he was overcome with emotion and fought back tears. As the room fell silent for a few moments, Jolene, Sally's attorney, was seated the closest to Jim and reached out to ask him if he was okay. Jim was able to collect himself and moved forward with the rest of the meeting.

Weeks later, after reaching a successful conclusion in their Collaborative divorce, Jim called his attorney to thank him for helping them through this difficult process. Jim specifically remembered the moment when he had nearly broken down in the meeting and the empathy Sally's attorney showed him. "Here I was, in the middle of a divorce I never wanted and my wife's attorney, someone I thought would be my worst enemy, is showing me the compassion I would expect from my best friend. I remember thinking, What kind of world had I entered? I was very grateful that I could feel so safe at such a difficult time."

CHAPTER 10

The Middle Four-Way Meetings

Now that you've finished the first four-way, we hope that you're feeling good about the process. You've met all the players and eased most of your fears, you know the rules, you experienced the give and take of information, and you understand what's expected of you as you move forward.

The first four-way meeting will produce several results—tangible and intangible—that will be important parts of your next meeting:

- Perceptions
- Impressions
- Minutes
- Agenda

Perceptions and Projections

It's very important that you discuss with your lawyer your subjective views of the first meeting: how you perceived your spouse's attorney; what made you feel relaxed and what made you feel ill at ease, and so on. Your lawyer, in turn, will be able to answer questions, clear up misunderstandings, give you a different perspective, and identify problems that need to be resolved for future meetings. You may have already shared some of your thoughts with your lawyer on your way to the parking lot after the meeting. But make sure you leave yourself plenty of time for a more detailed discussion as far in advance of the second meeting as possible.

Your lawyer also will want to know whether there have been any changes or significant events in your family situation since you last met. Tell your lawyer about any concerns you might have and anything else you think he should know. If two-way meetings with your spouse haven't been going well, your lawyer may suggest that you cut back or stop. If they are going well, your lawyer will probably suggest that you and your spouse get together more often.

Minutes

The minutes are a summary of everything that happened during the first meeting. They should include a list of homework assignments that were agreed upon. More importantly, they will contain the agenda for the next meeting.

Agenda

Second-meeting agenda items typically include long- and short-term resolution of issues having to do with the house, property valuation, parenting time, debt allocation, medical care, child support, and spousal support.

Put some real thought into setting the agenda—in terms of the subjects themselves—and the order in which they'll be discussed. It's often a good idea to start with a few less controversial items first. Getting a few issues resolved early can give you and your spouse a feeling of confidence in the process and a sense of accomplishment. Having those successes under your belt will make it easier to tackle more complicated and more emotionally charged issues. On the other hand, if there's a particular issue that's so heavy on your mind that you can't focus on anything else, by all means start with that one.

Discussing the Agenda with Your Attorney

Since you and your attorney know the issues to be discussed and the order in which they'll need to be dealt with, the two of you can go through them one by one. You'll of course want to discuss any legal implications. But most importantly you'll be able to practice articulating your wants and needs as interests. For example, if one item on the next meeting's agenda is medical insurance, a statement of interest might be: "I would like quality medical insurance for the family paid for in the most economical way." Having a few practice sessions with your attorney will give you the confidence to present your interests clearly and calmly.

Preparing for Subsequent Four-Ways

With your conferencing done, agenda studied, interests rehearsed, and homework completed, you're as ready as you'll ever be for the next four-way. The second meeting, and all of the those that follow, will proceed in the order dictated in the agenda created at the previous meeting.

If You Reach an Impasse

While the Collaborative process offers a forum for resolving most of your marital issues, every once in a while you'll run into something that you and your spouse just can't agree on. So what happens?

Well, in a lot of cases, the couple slips back into wrestling with positions instead of focusing on interests. It's your lawyers' job to get the discussions back on track.

Impasses can often be broken by the couple and their attorneys by doing a little brainstorming. The theory here is that if the parties are willing to work on finding solutions to the impasses, then it's not really an impasse. Brainstorming can involve presenting possible solutions as well as possible *interim* solutions, such as bringing in a mediator to shake up the settlement mix. (For example, the presence of a mediator obviously would change the configuration from four-way to five-way, which in itself should change the meeting dynamics and open new possibilities for settlement. Additionally, the mediator would become the facilitator and, as a neutral, be a little more directive with the clients.) It might also involve asking some of the neutral experts to participate in the discussions. This sometimes loosens things up enough for a few options to emerge.

CHAPTER 11

Working Toward Solutions in Between the Four-Way Meetings

Much of the success of the four-way meeting is dependent on what happens *in between*. With enough preparation, four-ways can go incredibly smoothly. Without preparation, they can be ineffective or, in the worse case, counterproductive. While there's no limit to what can happen in between your meetings, most of the work you do between your meetings will fall into one of the following categories:

- Debriefing with your attorney
- Taking care of yourself and restoring your emotional well-being
- Completing your homework assignments
- Having two-way meetings with your spouse
- Having other two-way meetings with your attorney
- Working with other team members
- Working with outside experts

Debriefing with Your Attorney

As a general rule, you should arrange to meet with your attorney as soon as possible after each meeting. Many attorneys set aside time to debrief immediately after each meeting. Others do it a little later. Talk this over with your attorney *before* each meeting so you can set aside the time you both need.

During your debriefing meeting, you'll have an opportunity to share with your lawyer your perceptions and ideas about how things went. If your expectations weren't met, or if things happened that you did not expect, tell your attorney so you can either adjust your expectations or develop a strategy to help the next meeting conform more closely to them. You should also review the homework that you agreed to complete before the next four-way meeting and make sure you understand it.

As part of your debriefing process you also can set aside time to take care of yourself so that you can restore the strength you need to move forward effectively.

Taking Care of Yourself

Even when the four-way meetings go smoothly, you'll probably walk out feeling tired and emotionally drained. The next steps will require renewed energy, so it's important that you set aside some time to take care of yourself to preserve and restore your physical, emotional, and spiritual strength. We often suggest to our clients that they schedule a purely self-indulgent activity the evening of each four-way meeting. How you choose to take care of yourself is up to you. But if you're looking for some suggestions, here are a number of things our clients have done:

- Schedule dinner with a good friend so that you can relax, have fun, or simply get some emotional support.
- Meet with your coach to talk about your emotional reaction to what happened.
- See your therapist and get some advice on how to cope with what's happening in your life. (But don't use this as an opportunity to get legal advice. Taking legal advice from a therapist and psychological counseling from your attorney is a common mistake that can inhibit your progress on both fronts.)
- Schedule time for prayer or mediation after the meeting.
- Take a walk through a park, along the beach, or in some other place where you feel peaceful and relaxed.

While finding the time to take care of yourself during the divorce process may seem difficult or even ridiculous, given everything that's going on, we can't emphasize enough how important it is. It's entirely possible that getting through the process successfully may depend more on self-care than on anything else. We often tell our clients that divorce is 80 percent emotional and 20 percent legal. Still, most people spend a lot more time and money on the 20 percent than on the 80.

As attorneys, we can't (and shouldn't) give you psychological advice. But we can assure you that, in our experience, clients who put some time into caring for themselves have far more successful legal outcomes.

Continuing success in the process requires both parties to function at high levels, at least during crucial negotiations. Divorcing parties face many obstacles that can impair their ability to function, resulting in depression, emotional disorders, and grieving over the loss of the relationship. If you're experiencing any emotional issues that are seriously affecting your ability to function, you absolutely *must* allow yourself enough time to work through them in between meetings. You will also need to take your mental state into account when scheduling meetings.

If you are severely depressed or haven't emotionally accepted the divorce, you may need to consider asking for more time before engaging in further negotiations. If the situation is reversed, you may be asked to be patient and allow your spouse adequate time to prepare him or herself emotionally to go forward.

Keeping Your Fears and Anxieties in Check

As you have probably already discovered, during a divorce, your mind has a tendency to work overtime. Racing and spinning all day, and sometimes all night, your mind can be so busy that it seems there's hardly space in your head for clear rational thinking. This, at a time when clear rational thinking is exactly what you need! So one of the things you can do to "get ready" for your divorce is to get and stay centered.

Stu, a practicing Buddhist, has found through the years that a practice he developed to help himself stay centered has been immensely helpful to some of our clients. It helps place the mind squarely in what he calls the "Serenity Space" (the site of clear rational thinking), keeping it out of the "Insecurity Space" (the site of all our busy, troubling thoughts). In preparation for the Collaborative process, try the Serenity Space practice, which is set out in full in Appendix I. You may find it helpful to keep your mind engaged in clear thinking as you move forward through the Collaborative process.

Completing Homework Assignments

Examples of homework include:

- Obtaining copies of bank or asset statements
- Getting an appraisal or market analysis of your home
- Working on your budget
- Getting together with your spouse to work on dividing household goods
- Looking up the blue-book values on your cars

The more of these mundane tasks you and your spouse do on your own, the more you'll be able to reduce your legal fees. But be careful not to take on more than you reasonably can. You may have less energy than you anticipate, and it's very important that you follow through on your commitments. So if there's a task that could be done more efficiently by your attorney or another member of your team, feel free to delegate. You may also find that you lack the time or emotional energy to complete certain tasks, even if they aren't technically difficult.

In addition, give yourself enough time to complete your tasks. Some clients who are in a hurry to get the divorce over with greatly underestimate the amount of time it will take them to do their homework. Not allowing yourself enough time can end up prolonging the process and increasing your expenses unnecessarily.

If you do find that you cannot complete your assignments on time, it's important to notify the other participants so a decision can be made about whether the next meeting needs to be postponed. This type of courtesy will go a long way toward building (or restoring) the trust necessary to achieve the best outcomes for your situation.

Two-Way Meetings Between You and Your Spouse

Some couples are very comfortable meeting on almost any issue and can, with very little direction from the attorneys, have very effective two-way meetings. Others find it very difficult even to be in the same room with each other, and will need to rely on other methods of communicating between meetings (phone conferences, e-mail, meeting in the presence of other people, and so on).

Many couples fall somewhere in between—they can meet on their own to resolve simpler issues, such as dividing the household goods, but can't address more complex or emotional issues without the presence of outside experts. If this is true in your case, decide which issues you can discuss and stick to those.

The critical factor in deciding whether to have a two-way meeting with your spouse is the existence (or lack) of a safe and effective environment. Similarly, there should never be any two-way negotiations unless both you and your spouse are completely willing to participate. Pressuring one party into a discussion when he or she is reluctant to engage may undermine the process and undo some of the valuable progress you may have made in the four-way meetings.

One particularly important ground rule is that both of you have the right to end the meeting *at any time,* as soon as it becomes unproductive or uncomfortable. There may be a time and place for you and your spouse to have emotional exchanges (such as in the presence of a counselor). However, allowing emotionally charged, unstructured negotiations to occur between you and your spouse without a professional present often can cause emotional reactions that make it difficult to move forward with the decisions you need to make.

Follow-up Two-Way Meetings with Your Attorney

In addition to your regularly scheduled postmeeting debriefings, you and your attorney will be in regular contact at other times, either in person, by phone, or through e-mail. As each four-way meeting approaches, you'll need to check in with your attorney to prepare. You'll also want to keep him or her up-to-date on your homework assignments, meetings with your spouse, or meetings with other team members or experts.

It's crucial that you stay in close communication with your attorney so that he or she can give you the direction that you need. But you'll have to judge for yourself what "in close communication" means. If you are in touch too often, you'll just be running up your bill, whereas if you're in touch too infrequently, you may end up causing delays and you may overlook some important options.

Working with Other Team Members

If you have chosen to add coaches, child specialists, financial neutrals, or other specialists to your team, you'll probably be meeting with them in between your four-way attorney meetings. In fact, if you and your spouse are both working with coaches, you may need to have regular four-ways with them in addition to the ones you have with your attorneys.

If one of your team members has been assigned the role of case manager (see chapter 4), stay in regular communication with him or her to make sure everyone knows about all of the meetings that are going on, regardless of who's participating. If you don't have a formal case manager, you'll need to find some other way (such as e-mail) to provide periodic scheduling and progress updates to everyone on the team.

If you've decided to use mediation along with the Collaborative process, you and your spouse may be meeting with the mediator in between the four-way attorney meetings.

Getting Advice from Friends and Family

One thing not to do: Don't share in-depth detail about your marital situation with friends or relatives without expecting a ton of advice on what *they* think you should do—and which you invariably will find you do *not* want to do. (Most of the insights from friends and neighbors come from their experience with *adversarial* divorce, i.e., advising you to take the money from your joint account and put it in your own account so your spouse can't get it. This type of action increases the level of fear between spouses and often results in the other party taking destructive countermeasures. Advice to unilaterally change the locks on the home is another example of bad counsel.)

Working with Outside Experts

It is likely you will be working with outside experts on various issues. Once again, the key issues will be keeping everyone up-to-date and everything on schedule.

The hard work you do in between the meetings will pay off during each of the following four-way meetings. It will also help you achieve your most important goals.

What If Collaboration Fails?

In a small percentage of Collaborative cases, the parties fail to reach a settlement and the process falls apart. These rare occurrences seem to fall into two categories:

1. Couples who participate fully in the Collaborative process but end up unable to reach an agreement on one or more issues. In some cases it's possible to restart the Collaborative process or take other steps short of going to court.

2. One of the parties unilaterally terminates the Collaboration midstream. In these cases there's virtually no chance of preserving any of the agreements that may have been reached, and the couple is headed for litigation. Why does this happen? In our experience, the spouse who pulls the plug had not committed him or herself enough to the process to ride out the rough spots.

So what happens when the Collaborative process is terminated? In accordance with the terms of the Participation Agreement, the two Collaborative lawyers withdraw from the case. The parties, if they intend to proceed to litigation, which is usually the case, would retain trial lawyers, who will start preparing their cases. While most of the factual documents (financial statements, real estate and business valuations, and so on) produced as part of the Collaborative proceedings can be used in the court process, the conversations and agreements reached in the Collaborative settlement are not admissible in court. Some opinions by neutral experts may be used in court, but only if the parties and the experts agree.

It's truly a sad event when the Collaborative process breaks down. We know from our own experience that the path to court is difficult and painful for everyone involved. When this happens, we feel like a couple of old prospectors watching some tenderfeet head off on a hazardous trail, heedless of our warnings.

Enough talk of failure. With commitment and perseverance by you, your spouse, and your Collaborative professionals, you will reach agreement on all your issues and be ready for the final closing steps. If you have been successful in working through all of your issues, you are now ready for your final four-way meeting, in which you will finalize the main part of the Collaborative process.

CHAPTER 12

The Final Four-Way Meeting and Other Closing Steps

When you and your spouse have reached agreements on all of your marital issues, it's time to schedule a final four-way meeting.

Signing a Stipulation

At some point during one of the middle four-way meetings, one of your attorneys will draft a Stipulation (sometimes called a Marital Termination Agreement). The Stipulation contains your entire written agreement, including custodial arrangement for the children or Parenting Plan; child support terms; who claims which children for tax exemptions; health insurance and medical and dental costs for the children; health insurance for a spouse, spousal maintenance or waiver of it; division of marital assets, including real property; allocation of income taxes in final year of marriage; division of household goods; allocation of debts; and provisions for designation of life insurance proceeds. Each Stipulation is tailored to include any other specific agreements the parties have made as part of their process. Sometimes the full agreement is read out loud and/or reviewed during the last four-way meeting.

Before signing it, make sure you have thoroughly reviewed all of the terms and that all of your questions have been answered. If you have any last-minute corrections or changes, make them now. It's vital that you fully understand the Stipulation, and that it clearly reflects your interests. The Stipulation is often reviewed and revised at the four-way meetings and, once everyone approves the language, they sign it and file it with the court.

While it's possible to sign the Stipulation outside of one of the four-ways, we recommend that you do so during a meeting. This allows everyone a last chance to make changes with everyone present.

Reaching Closure

The other advantage of signing the papers at a final meeting is that it creates an event that can give some formal closure to the process. Throughout the process it is common for the parties to express a strong desire to be finished. However, it's not always clear when, exactly, "finished" actually happens, since there are several stages in the process that could be seen as being the final step.

Until fairly recently, most courts held a final hearing in which one or both of the parties appeared in front of a judge to approve the final papers. Today, that hearing is often waived, and the signed Stipulation is considered the final legal act performed by either party prior to the divorce. The Stipulation is a contract that, once signed, will play a large role in guiding your future. While it is, in many ways, simply a blueprint for that future, it has great legal and emotional significance.

Acknowledging the Final Moments

Even clients who have been eager to get the divorce over with often experience mixed emotions when they sign the final documents. While you may feel ready to move forward with your new life and you may believe that you have fully grieved the breakdown of the marriage, signing the final documents often resurrects feelings of sadness and loss.

When signing these final papers, many people choose to honor the significance of the event in some manner. We've had some clients choose to say a few words of closure. Others actually have brought in cake and champagne as a symbol of the joy of being able to move on after a long period of pain.

Occasionally the newly divorced couple requests a ceremony to symbolize the end of their marriage relationship and the start of their new phase of life. These larger closing ceremonies or rituals usually are done outside of the four-ways, but it's certainly possible to have one during the last meeting. Either way, it's common to at least discuss and plan a portion of the closing ceremony at the final four-way.

One of our clients designed a very moving service with witnesses and a written script. For our part, the lawyers brought an ivy plant and two pots to the ceremony. We asked the parties to divide the plant in two, and each take one pot home. Ceremonies are becoming more common in Collaborative divorces. After all, marriage is replete with symbolic words and acts. Ceremonies designed by the parties can help bring closure to the marriage and signal the beginning of a new phase of their relationship. *A Healing Divorce* by Phil Penningroth and Barbara Penningroth is an excellent book on the subject.

Most religions have a tradition for marriage-closure ceremonies.

The Collaborative process is a legal process and is not, by itself, recognized as a religious event in this manner. However, it is possible for couples to reach agreements to cooperate with annulments or *gittin*.

Choosing a Closure Event

Some people choose not to have a final four-way meeting at all because of the discomfort or pain of being with their spouse during this event. Whether you choose to acknowledge the final event of the dissolution is purely a matter of personal choice and may depend on, among other things, your spiritual or religious affiliation. You should communicate your ideas about how you want to handle the closure of your divorce so that you and your spouse can agree on handling the final steps in a manner that best suits your interests.

Divorcing with Dignity

One of the intangible benefits of the Collaborative method is the opportunity to preserve the dignity of your relationship in the way you approach your divorce. From our discussions with numerous clients over the years, we have found that those who maintained their divorce with dignity were better prepared for what lay ahead in their lives, including their new relationships.

As you take your next steps into a new stage of your life's journey, we hope that the experiences of the Collaborative process have taught you far more than simply how to achieve the best outcome in your divorce. We hope you will see, as we have, that the principles that make the Collaborative process effective are closely related to principles and values that can make a difference in every aspect of our lives.

CHAPTER 13

Putting the Divorce Behind You and Nurturing Your Family's Postdivorce Life

Collectively, we have practiced family law for nearly half a century. And we've both had the opportunity to reconnect with some of our clients years—even decades—after their divorces. Their stories have covered the spectrum, but often fall into one of three categories:

- The client who never really recovers from the enormous setback of the divorce
- The client who maintains a life very similar to his or her life predivorce
- The client who emerges from this painful experience stronger than ever before

Over the years it's become increasingly clear that the decisions our clients made during their divorce had a tremendous impact on how they reshaped their lives. The responsibility and the credit for those decisions belong primarily to them. But it has been our personal mission to do whatever we can to help clients make choices that will allow them to move on to a better life than the one they had previously known.

The Difference That Collaborative Law Has Made

The concept of Collaborative law, and its development over the last fifteen years, has created opportunities for positive resolutions to often difficult and complicated situations in a way that no one—except for Stu—would have ever dreamed possible. The Collaborative option is, for those who choose to make the most of it, a better way, a way to help you rebuild your life that allows you to preserve the good that still exists in your family while helping you to attain your highest goals in the divorce. We are enormously impressed by the clients we've seen who find the strength to work through their issues in the Collaborative process in a way that offers them, and, in most cases, their children, an opportunity to improve their lives immeasurably. It is an honor to work with these people, and it has been an honor to share both our expertise and the wisdom of our many brave clients with you.

The great psychologist Viktor Frankl, who spent four years in a Nazi concentration camp, observed that no matter what is taken from a person, "the last of the human freedoms [is] to choose one's attitude in any given set of circumstances, to choose one's own way." This philosophy is at the heart of the Collaborative process. It's our great hope that you and your spouse will join the growing number of divorcing couples who have recognized that they have the power to choose the outcome of their divorce.

When Are You Done?

Although your marriage may be over, your divorce itself isn't. If you have children, you certainly can see that the foundation that you created in your Collaborative divorce will make a difference throughout the rest of your life. But even if you don't have children and have no legal obligation to ever see your ex-spouse again, don't underestimate the impact that your divorce had and will have in your life. For most people, divorce is a life-changing event. And if you have fully grieved the loss of the marriage, the experiences of your marriage and your divorce are likely to reverberate throughout your lives, like a wave in the ocean.

So how do couples who complete this Collaborative process function in their postdivorce lives? The only generality we can make is that the lessons learned in the Collaborative process and the degree to which a couple has taken responsibility and embraced this process makes all the difference in charting how they will relate to and manage their lives and family relations in the future.

We have seen couples who start the Collaborative process unable to speak to or even look at each other move toward easy communication—even working together outside the confines of the four-way conference. Overall, we've seen that a couple's postdivorce relationship is a product of how they conducted themselves during the divorcing process.

There are times, however, when circumstances are such that modifications in the divorce decree may be desired by one of the parties. These are called *postdecree modifications*. In the litigation model (going to court), the parties, often still angry and bitter, can use postdecree hearings as a way of harassing the other and keeping the divorce process alive. Sometimes the issue is a legitimate one, but it has to be dealt with in court because the parties are unable to find a way to communicate productively to resolve the issue. With the Collaborative model, you are way ahead of the game. Communication should be in place and if a modification needs to be addressed, your Collaborative team is ready to assist you.

When we introduce ourselves socially as divorce lawyers, people often seem surprised to learn that we've chosen a career that requires us to spend a large portion of the day working with people who are going through some of the worst times of their lives. They'll say, "It's hard to imagine why you'd want to work around so much pain."

But divorce represents both an end and a beginning. What makes the practice of Collaborative law fulfilling for us is the ability to help people focus on creating a fresh start, a new life, a happier situation. A divorce lawyer's job is similar to an emergency room doctor's. If the doctor focused only on the tragedy that brought a patient into his or her care, he or she would find the job impossible to bear. But if the doctor is able to accept the past and see his or her role in that person's life as a means to recovery and healing, the job is seen as a blessing and a reward.

Working in divorce law is much the same. Every day, people who are injured find their way into our offices and lives, and eventually they leave on a path of progress and healing. We hope that for you the end of this book will mark the beginning of a new—and better—stage of your life's journey.

PART FIVE

Appendices

APPENDIX A

COLLABORATIVE LAW PARTICIPATION AGREEMENT

Dissolution with Children

AMONG:

_____Participant—Husband/Father

-and-

_____Attorney for Husband/Father

-and-

_____Participant—Wife/Mother

-and-

_____Attorney for Wife/Mother

1.0 GOALS

1.1. We, the Participants, believe that it is in our best interests and the best interests of our minor child(ren) to reach an agreement through the Collaborative process instead of going to Court.

1.2. We agree to use the Collaborative Law process to resolve differences. Collaborative Law is based on:

- honesty (full and complete disclosure of all assets, debts, and income);
- satisfying the interests of both parties;
- cooperation;
- integrity;

- professionalism;
- dignity;
- respect; and
- candor.

1.3. Collaborative Law focuses on our **future** well-being and the future well-being of our child(ren).

1.4. Collaborative Law does **not** rely on Court-imposed solutions.

1.5. Our goals are:

- to resolve our differences in the best interests of our child(ren);
- to eliminate the negative economic, social, and emotional consequences of litigation; and
- to find solutions that are acceptable to both of us.

2.0 WE WILL NOT GO TO COURT

2.1. **Out-of-Court**. We commit ourselves to settling this case without going to Court.

2.2. **Disclosure**. We agree to give full and complete disclosure of all information whether requested or not. Any request for disclosure of information will be made informally. We will provide this information promptly.

We acknowledge that by using the Collaborative process we are giving up certain investigative procedures and methods that would be available to us in the litigation process. We give up these measures with the specific understanding that we will make full and fair disclosure of all assets, income, debts, and other information necessary for a fair settlement. Participation in the Collaborative Law process, and the settlement reached, is based upon the assumption that we have acted in good faith and have provided complete and accurate information to the best of our ability. We may be required to sign a sworn statement containing a full and fair disclosure of our incomes, assets, and debts.

2.3. **Settlement conferences**. We agree to engage in informal discussions and conferences to settle all issues. All communication during settlement meetings will focus on the property, financial, and parenting issues in the dissolution and the constructive resolution of those issues. We are free to discuss issues in the dissolution with each other outside of the settlement meetings if we both agree and are comfortable doing so. We are also free to insist that these discussions be reserved for the settlement meetings where both attorneys are present.

Each of us promises not to spring discussions on the other in unannounced telephone calls or in surprise visits to the other's residence.

We understand and acknowledge that the costs for settlement meetings are substantial and require everyone's cooperation to make the best possible use of available resources. To achieve this goal, we agree not to engage in unnecessary discussions of past events.

2.4. **Communication**. We acknowledge that inappropriate communications regarding our dissolution can be harmful to our child(ren). Communication with our child(ren) regarding the dissolution will occur only if it is appropriate and done by mutual agreement or with the advice of a child specialist. We specifically agree that our child(ren) will not be included in any discussion regarding the dissolution except as described in this Agreement.

3.0. CAUTIONS

We understand and acknowledge the following:

3.1. **Commitment**. There is no guarantee we will successfully resolve our differences using the Collaborative Law process. Success is primarily dependent upon our commitment to the process. We also understand that this process cannot eliminate concerns about any disharmony, distrust, or irreconcilable differences that have lead to our marriage dissolution.

3.2. **Legal issues**. The Collaborative Law process is designed to resolve the following legal issues:

- Parenting time;
- Financial support of our child(ren), including unreimbursed medical and dental expenses of our minor child(ren), and day-care costs, if any;

- Insurance (medical, dental, life);
- Spousal maintenance;
- Division of property and debts;
- Nonmarital property;
- Attorneys' fees and costs;
- and other issues we may agree to address.

This process is not designed to address therapeutic or psychological issues. When these or other nonlegal issues arise, our attorneys may refer us to appropriate experts or consultants.

3.3. **Attorney role**. Although we pledge to be respectful and to negotiate in an interest-based manner, we are each entitled to assert our respective interests, and our attorneys will help us do this in a productive manner. We understand that our attorneys have a professional duty to represent his or her own client diligently and is not the attorney for the other, even though our attorneys share a commitment to the Collaborative Law process.

4.0. ATTORNEYS' FEES AND COSTS

We agree that our attorneys are entitled to be paid for their services. We also agree that each of us will pay our own attorney unless otherwise agreed during the Collaborative Law process that one of us will contribute to the other's attorney fees or that marital assets will be used to pay both attorneys' fees.

5.0. PARTICIPATION WITH INTEGRITY

5.1. We will respect each other.

5.2. We will work to protect the privacy and dignity of everyone involved in the Collaborative Law process.

5.3. We will maintain a high standard of integrity and specifically shall not take advantage of any miscalculations or mistakes of others, but shall immediately identify and correct them.

6.0. EXPERTS

6.1. We agree to use neutral experts for any issue that requires expert advice and/or recommendation.

6.2. We will retain any expert jointly unless we agree otherwise in writing.

6.3. We will agree in advance as to the source of payment for the experts' retainers or other fees.

6.4. We agree to direct all experts to assist us in resolving our differences without litigation.

6.5. Unless otherwise agreed in writing, the neutral expert and any report, recommendation, or documents generated by, or any oral communication from, the neutral expert shall be shared with each of us and our respective attorneys and covered by the confidentiality clause of this Agreement.

7.0. CHILD(REN)'S ISSUES

7.1. We agree to act quickly to resolve differences related to our child(ren).

7.2. We agree to promote a caring, loving, and involved relationship between our child(ren) and each parent.

7.3. We agree to work for the best interests of the family as a whole.

7.4. We agree not to involve our child(ren) in our differences.

7.5. We agree not to remove our minor child(ren) from the State of Minnesota without the prior written consent of the other while the Collaborative Law process is pending.

8.0. WE WILL NEGOTIATE IN GOOD FAITH

8.1. We acknowledge that each attorney represents only one client in the Collaborative Law process.

8.2. We understand that this process will involve good faith negotiation, with complete and honest disclosure.

8.3. We will be expected to take a balanced approach to resolving all differences. Where our interests differ, we will each use our best efforts to create proposals that are acceptable to both of us.

8.4. None of us will use threats of litigation as a way of forcing settlement, although each of us may discuss the likely outcome of going to Court.

9.0. RIGHTS AND OBLIGATIONS PENDING SETTLEMENT

We acknowledge the signing of a Joint Petition for the purpose of commencing a dissolution of marriage proceeding. Although we have agreed to work outside the judicial system, we agree to be bound by the following notices as if a Summons had been served on each of us:

NOTICE OF TEMPORARY RESTRAINING AND
ALTERNATIVE DISPUTE RESOLUTION PROVISIONS

UNDER MINNESOTA LAW, SERVICE OF THIS SUMMONS MAKES THE FOLLOWING REQUIREMENTS APPLY TO BOTH PARTIES TO THIS ACTION, UNLESS THEY ARE MODIFIED BY THE COURT OR THE PROCEEDING IS DISMISSED:

(1) NEITHER PARTY WILL DISPOSE OF ANY ASSETS EXCEPT (i) FOR THE NECESSITIES OF LIFE OR FOR THE NECESSARY GENERATION OF INCOME OR PRESERVATION OF ASSETS, (ii) BY AN AGREEMENT IN WRITING, OR (iii) TO RETAIN COUNSEL TO CARRY ON OR TO CONTEST THIS PROCEEDING.

(2) NEITHER PARTY MAY HARASS THE OTHER PARTY.

(3) ALL CURRENTLY AVAILABLE INSURANCE COVERAGE MUST BE MAINTAINED WITHOUT CHANGE IN COVERAGE OR BENEFICIARY DESIGNATION.

IF YOU VIOLATE OF ANY OF THESE PROVISIONS, YOU WILL BE SUBJECT TO SANCTIONS BY THE COURT.

10.0. ABUSE OF THE COLLABORATIVE LAW PROCESS

We understand that both attorneys must withdraw from this case if either attorney learns that either of us has taken unfair advantage of this process. Some examples are:

- abusing our child(ren);
- planning or threatening to flee the jurisdiction of the Court with our child(ren);
- disposing of property without the consent of the other;
- withholding or misrepresenting relevant information;
- failing to disclose the existence or true nature of assets, income, or debts;
- failing to participate collaboratively in this process; or
- any action to undermine or take unfair advantage of the Collaborative Law process

11.0. ENFORCEABILITY OF AGREEMENTS

11.1. **Temporary agreements**. In the event either of us requires a temporary agreement for any purpose, the agreement will be put in writing and signed by us and our attorneys. Any written temporary agreement is considered to be made pursuant to a commenced dissolution proceeding and therefore can be submitted to the Court as a basis for an Order and enforced, if necessary.

11.2. **Permanent agreement**. Any final, permanent agreement (sometimes called a Joint Petition and Stipulation or Marital Termination Agreement) we sign shall be submitted to the Court as the basis for entry of a Judgment and Decree of Dissolution.

11.3. **In case of withdrawal**. If either of us or either attorney withdraws from the Collaborative Law process, any written temporary agreement may be presented to the Court as a basis for an Order pursuant to a dissolution proceeding, which the Court may make retroactive to the date of the written agreement. Similarly, in the event of a withdrawal from the Collaborative Law process, any final agreement may be presented to the Court as a basis for entry of a Judgment and Decree of Dissolution.

12.0. LEGAL PROCESS

12.1. **Pleadings**. Other than the signing of a Joint Petition to commence a dissolution of marriage proceeding, neither of us or our attorneys will file the Joint Petition with the Court, nor will we permit any motion or document to be served or filed that would initiate court intervention during the Collaborative Law process pending final agreement.

12.2. **Stipulation**. After we reach a final agreement, one of the attorneys will prepare a Stipulation (sometimes called a Marital Termination Agreement) for review and signature by our attorneys and us.

12.3. **No court**. None of us will use the Court during the Collaborative Law process.

12.4. **Participant withdrawal from Collaborative Law process**. If one of us decides to withdraw from the process, s/he shall provide prompt written notice to his or her attorney, who in turn will promptly notify the other attorney in writing.

12.5. **Attorney withdrawal**. If one of our attorneys decides to withdraw from the process, s/he will promptly notify their client and the other attorney in writing.

12.6. **Waiting period**. Upon withdrawal from the process, there will be a thirty-day waiting period, absent an emergency, before the scheduling of any court hearing, to permit us to retain new counsel and to make an orderly transition.

12.7. **Previous agreements**. All temporary agreements will remain in full force and effect during the thirty-day period.

12.8. **No surprise**. The intent of this section is to avoid surprise and prejudice to the rights of the nonwithdrawing participant.

12.9. **Presentation to Court**. Accordingly, we agree that either of us may bring this provision to the attention of the Court in requesting the continuance of a hearing scheduled by the other or his/her attorney during the thirty-day waiting period.

13.0 DISQUALIFICATION

13.1. **Withdrawal of attorney**. If either Collaborative Law attorney withdraws from the case, the other attorney must also withdraw unless a withdrawing attorney is replaced by another Collaborative Law attorney who agrees in writing to comply with this Participation Agreement.

13.2. **Disqualification in subsequent matters**. After termination of the Collaborative Law process, whether by settlement or termination before settlement, neither attorney shall represent his or her client in a subsequent non-Collaborative matter against the other party.

14.0. CONFIDENTIALITY

14.1. **Confidentiality**. All settlement proposals exchanged within the Collaborative Law process will be confidential and without prejudice. If subsequent litigation occurs, we agree:

    a. That we will not introduce, as evidence in Court, information disclosed during the Collaborative Law process for the purpose of reaching a settlement, except documents otherwise compellable by law, including any sworn statements as to financial status made by us;

    b. That we will not introduce, as evidence in Court, information disclosed during the Collaborative Law process with respect to the other's behavior or legal position during the process;

    c. That we will not attempt to depose either attorney or neutral expert, or ask or subpoena either attorney or any neutral expert to testify in any court proceeding with regard to matters disclosed during the Collaborative Law process; and

    d. That we will not require the production at any court proceeding of any notes, records, or documents in the attorney's possession or in the possession of any neutral expert. However, once discharged, the attorneys shall return the file to their respective clients, excluding attorney work product.

14.2. **Applicability**. We agree this Confidentiality provision applies to any subsequent litigation, arbitration, or any other method of alternative dispute resolution.

15.0. ACKNOWLEDGMENT

15.1. We and our attorneys acknowledge that we have read this Agreement, understand its terms and conditions, and agree to abide by them.

15.2. We understand that by agreeing to this alternative method of resolving our dissolution issues, we are giving up certain rights, including the right to formal discovery, formal court hearings, and other procedures provided by the adversarial legal system.

15.3. We have chosen the Collaborative Law process to reduce emotional and financial costs, and to generate a final agreement that addresses our concerns. We agree to work in good faith to achieve these goals.

16.0. PLEDGE

WE HEREBY PLEDGE TO COMPLY WITH AND TO PROMOTE THE SPIRIT AND WRITTEN WORD OF THIS PARTICIPATION AGREEMENT.

Dated: _____   Dated: _____

WIFE'S NAME, ADDRESS   HUSBAND'S NAME, ADDRESS

_____   _____

Attorney for Wife (   )   Attorney for Husband (   )
ADDRESS, PHONE   ADDRESS, PHONE
FAX   FAX

APPENDIX B

List of Common Marital Issues

The following is a list of some of the issues that may be considered as part of a dissolution. It is not necessary to reach agreements on all of these issues. However, it is helpful to at least consider the advantages of reaching agreements in each applicable area.

A. PARENTING AGREEMENT
1. Time-sharing schedule
   a. School year
   b. School breaks
   c. Holidays
   d. Parent and child birthdays
   e. Vacations with children
   f. Vacations without children
   g. Time with extended family members
   h. Schedule changes

2. Telephone access

3. Transportation

   4. Legal custody

   5. Decision Making
       a. Categories
           1) Education
           2) Health
           3) Child care
           4) Activities
           5) Religion
           6) Motor vehicles
           7) Other
       b. Procedure

   6. Communication/Information sharing

   7. Religious training

   8. Moving beyond present geographical area

   9. Periodic review

B. FINANCIAL SUPPORT

   1. Child support

   2. Spousal support

   3. Postsecondary education costs

   4. Responsibility for children's expenses
       a. Uninsured medical/dental/vision costs
       b. Activities
       c. Clothing
       d. Other

   5. Periodic review

C. HEALTH INSURANCE

D. LIFE INSURANCE ON EACH SPOUSE

E. FAMILY HOME

F. OTHER REAL ESTATE

G. HOUSEHOLD GOODS AND OTHER PERSONAL PROPERTY

H. VEHICLES

I. BUSINESS OWNERSHIP INTERESTS

J. STOCKS AND BONDS

K. BANK ACCOUNTS

L. OTHER ASSETS

M. OUTSTANDING DEBTS

N. RETIREMENT
1. Pension and profit-sharing plans

2. IRA accounts

3. Other

O. TAX ISSUES
1. Dependent deductions

2. Child-care deductions

3. Filing for current year
   a. Separate or joint
   b. Disposition of refund
   c. Responsibility for balance owed

4. Capital gain taxes

P. ATTORNEYS' FEES

Q. FUTURE MEDIATION CLAUSE

R. TEMPORARY ARRANGEMENTS
1. Housing

2. Parenting

3. Financial support

4. Managing assets and debts

S. OTHER

APPENDIX C

Sample Letter to Spouse

[Date]

Dear Dr. _____:

As you perhaps know, I have been contacted by your wife, _____, to represent her in marriage dissolution proceedings. I am writing you to outline the way I operate in these proceedings. My motivation is to try to enlist your active involvement in a refreshing approach to resolving dissolution issues that is straightforward and does not involve courts in any advocacy way.

The approach is called "Collaborative Law," and enclosed is a brochure describing the process. How it works is that each of you engages attorneys to represent you in the dissolution with the understanding that in the event that advocacy proceedings are required because you and your lawyers are not able to resolve the dissolution issues through informal talks and sharing of information, the Collaborative lawyers will withdraw and trial lawyers will be retained for the latter proceedings. What Collaborative Law does is interpose a "settlement" process between the parties and expensive and time-consuming trial procedures.

_____obviously is receptive to a Collaborative approach, as she has contacted me to represent her. If you should retain a Collaborative lawyer, we can proceed on that basis. Enclosed is a list of local family-law lawyers who will take cases on a Collaborative basis.

A Collaborative approach requires each of the parties to approach settlement with at least a little bit of "goodwill."

I hope you will consider this approach, as it has the possibility of saving time, money, and stress.

We are at a crossroads of some sort here that requires a choice on your part. Should you choose an advocacial attorney or choose not to take the next step in moving the process along, then I will advise _____ that I will not be able to represent her and recommend that she retain a trial attorney to advance her rights in court.

Should you care to do so, I would be most happy to meet with you at no charge and answer any questions you might have about the Collaborative process. In any event, I would appreciate hearing from you as to how you intend to proceed by [Date] so I can appropriately advise _____. Thank you.

Very truly yours,
Stuart G. Webb

APPENDIX D

Checklist of Attorney Questions

Choosing an attorney is largely a matter of personal preference and you should focus on the characteristics that matter the most to you. The purpose of this checklist is simply to help you think about the wide range of questions that you may have of your attorney. Many of these questions can be answered through your prospective attorney's Web site, brochures, or sample fee agreements. Other questions may need to be asked during your interview of the attorney.

QUESTIONS RELATED TO EXPERIENCE

How much experience does the attorney have?
How much experience do they have in family law?
How much experience do they have in Collaborative Law?
Are they experienced in mediation and other forms of dispute resolution?
Do they have trial experience?

QUESTIONS RELATED TO COSTS

Fees

What is their hourly rate?
What is the lowest increment of time that they will charge? (i.e., ¼ hour? ¹⁄₁₀ hour?)
Is there some work by the attorney that is not charged? What work?

Is the rate negotiable?
Is their rate subject to change?

Expenses

What expenses will you have to pay, in addition to their hourly rate? (i.e., filing fees, copy costs, postage costs, etc.)
How will these expenses be charged?

Retainer

How much is their retainer (up-front payment)?
Is the retainer negotiable?
Is the retainer refundable?
Does the retainer have to be replenished when it is used up?

Billing practices

How often do they send out bills?
How much detail is shown on the statement?

Staff

What support staff does the attorney have available? (i.e., paralegals, recep-
tionist, associates, etc.)
What hourly rate is charged for each staff member?
Who else will work on your case? What portion of their work will be charged?

General cost-saving issues

Are there some things you can do to keep costs down? What are some recommendations?

QUESTIONS RELATED TO AFFILIATION

Are they members of professional organizations? Have they been recognized by those organizations?

QUESTIONS RELATED TO PHILOSOPHY

What is their philosophy in relation to family law?

Do they have any preferences, values, or personal beliefs that could affect the type of advice that they give?

QUESTIONS RELATED TO TRAINING/EDUCATION

How much Collaborative training do they have?

How much mediation training do they have?

Do they have other specialized legal training?

Do they have any specialized training outside of law? (i.e., accounting, psychology, a particular language or culture, etc.)

QUESTIONS RELATED TO WORKLOAD/TIMELINESS

Do they currently have room for another case?

Do they ever turn down cases when they are too full?

Will you be forced to deal with an associate during a large portion of your representation?

Do they have any extended vacations or other matters coming up in the near future that could affect their availability?

How long does it typically take to get in for an appointment?

QUESTIONS RELATED TO EXPERIENCE IN YOUR COMMUNITY

What is their experience in your community?

Are they familiar with the specific procedures in your jurisdiction?

Are they familiar with many of the other attorneys or other possible team members in your community?

QUESTIONS RELATED TO TECHNOLOGY

Do they use e-mail? Do they check it regularly?

Do they have voice mail?

Can you fill out some of their information electronically?

Do they use spreadsheets?

What other software or equipment might be used in their case?

QUESTIONS RELATED TO SPECIFIC ISSUES IN YOUR CASE

If your case presents issues that you believe may require specialized knowledge (i.e., a complex business, a significant disability or health issue, a cultural issue), you may want to ask if your attorney has experience or training in that particular area.

QUESTIONS RELATED TO THE OTHER ATTORNEY OR TEAM MEMBERS (IF THE OTHER ATTORNEY OR TEAM MEMBER HAS BEEN DESIGNATED)

Are they familiar with the other attorney that your spouse has hired or is considering hiring?

If so, what has their experience been?

QUESTIONS RELATING TO ACHIEVEMENTS/RECOGNITIONS

Do they have any recognitions, awards, etc., that relate to their legal ability?

QUESTIONS RELATING TO PUBLISHED ARTICLES

Have they published articles or books relating to family law?

MISCELLANEOUS QUESTIONS

Do they have any references?

Do they have their clients complete questionnaires after each case? How long have they had that practice?

Do they have other relevant experiences? (i.e., teaching, writing, speaking, etc.)

What is their ideal type of client?

What types of clients do they find to be difficult?

APPENDIX E

Examples of Common Goals and Interests in Divorce Cases

To further help you distinguish interests or goals from positions, and to help you think about your own goals, we have provided the following list of common goals or interests that clients have expressed in divorce cases.

GOALS AND INTERESTS RELATING TO CHILDREN

Because the presence of children (particularly minor children) has a significant impact on the goals and interests in the divorce, we have separated this section into two categories, depending on whether the goals relate to the needs of children.

If you have children, it may be relatively easy to think about some general things that you want for your children. Here some examples to consider.

General goals relating to the general well-being of your children

- I want our children to be well-adjusted.
- I want our children to be happy.
- I want our children to feel good about themselves.

Goals relating to providing consistent parenting care

- I want my spouse and me to provide consistent care for our children.

- I want my spouse and me to have consistent discipline, expectations, consequences, curfews, chores, bedtimes, etc.
- I want my spouse and me to have the same parenting rules in both houses.
- I want my spouse and me to support each other in our parenting decisions.

Goals relating to parenting skills
- I want to develop better parenting skills.
- I want my spouse to develop better parenting skills.
- I want to have a better understanding of what children need when going through a divorce.

Goals relating to the allocation of parenting time
- I want our children to have meaningful contact with both parents.
- I do not want to be away from the children for more than four days at a time.

Goals relating to decision making
- I want to participate in major decisions affecting the lives of our children.

Goals relating to keeping the children free from conflict
- I want our children to be free from the conflict in the divorce.
- I do not want our children to believe they have to report to one parent about the other parent.
- I want to avoid having financial issues spill over to our parenting.
- I do not want our children to feel that they have to do anything to reject either parent.
- I want our children to feel comfortable talking about whether they enjoyed their time at both parents' homes.

Goals relating to the relationship the children will have with other adults

- I want our children to have appropriate relationships with new partners or stepparents.
- I want to make sure new adults are not introduced into the lives of the children until the children are ready.

Goals relating to flexibility in scheduling

- I want to have enough flexibility in the parenting schedule so that we can adjust the schedule to meet the needs of the children.
- I want to be able to move the residence of the minor children.

Goals relating to stability

- I want the parenting schedule to provide stability for the children.
- I want the parenting schedule to be predictable.
- I want to make sure each parent honors the agreed-upon schedule.
- I want the children to live near both parents.
- I want the children to be able to stay in their current school district.

Goals relating to communication with the other parent

- I want to be able to communicate effectively with the other parent regarding changes in schedule, updates on health, school, activities, consistent parenting rules, etc.
- I want to develop better communication skills.
- I want both parents to have access to information relating to school, medical issues, etc.
- I want to have regularly scheduled communication.
- I want both parents to honor ground rules for respectful communication.

Goals relating to communication with the children

- I want both parents to be able to communicate regularly with each child by phone and e-mail.
- I want all communication around our children to be respectful.
- I do not want our children to hear negative things about one parent from the other parent.

Goals relating to child care

- I want to minimize outside child care.
- I want to maintain high-quality child care.
- I want both parents to share in child-care decisions.

Goals relating to religion or spirituality

- I want our children to be raised in their current religion.
- I want our children to regularly attend religious services.
- I want both parents involved in the religious activities of our children.

Goals relating to medical care/physical health

- I want our children to have a good diet.
- I want our children to get adequate exercise.
- I want both parents to have full access to good medical/dental care.
- I want both parents to be able to attend medical appointments.
- I want both parents to share care of our children when they are sick.

Goals relating to education

- I want our children to be able to continue with their current schooling.
- I want both parents to participate in their school conferences/ activities.
- I want our children to attend _____ school.
- I want our children to maintain their current grades.
- I want our children to attend college.

- I want both parents to support the same educational goals.
- I want both parents to participate in our children's homework.

Goals relating to activities, music lessons, sports, etc.

- I want our children to remain in their current activities.
- I want both parents to agree on the future activities for our children and to support those activities.

Goals relating to vacations

- I want both parents to be able to take vacations with our children.

Goals relating to cultural heritage

- I want to make sure our children are raised according to their cultural heritage.

Goals relating to children's general financial issues

- I want our children to maintain their predivorce lifestyle in both homes.
- I want our children to be financially responsible.
- I want to make sure we set aside money to provide for college.
- I want to have an agreement about how we will pay for college for our children.

Goals relating to child-expense sharing

- I want both parents to share in the children's expenses based on their incomes.
- I want to find a way of sharing expenses that is easy to manage.

GOALS AND INTERESTS THAT DO NOT INVOLVE CHILDREN

Financial goals

- I want to be able to maintain my current lifestyle.
- I want to be able to own a home similar to the home we lived in during the marriage.
- I want to maintain a lifestyle that is equal to the lifestyle that my spouse will live.
- I want to be able to retire at age _____.
- I do not want to have to work outside the home until _____.
- I do not want to have to work full time until _____.
- I do not want to have to work outside the home at any time in the future.
- I want to be able to start a new career.
- I want to be able to pursue a career that I enjoy.
- I do not want to have to work overtime.
- I want to have more free time.
- I want to get out of debt.
- I want to learn how to live within my means.
- I want to learn how to manage money.
- I want to know how to budget.
- I want to understand investment.
- I want to learn skills for staying out of debt.
- I want my spouse to learn how to live within his/her means.
- I want my spouse to learn to manage money.
- I want to keep the costs of the divorce down.
- I want to be able to restore my credit.
- I want to reduce our tax obligation.
- I want a financial settlement that will last (is durable).

Vocational goals

- I want to become more educated.
- I want to learn a skill.
- I want to be able to choose the work I do.
- I want to be able to change careers at some point.

Personal/emotional goals

- I want to resolve the divorce issues with dignity.
- I want to keep our divorce issues private.
- I want to maintain a respectful relationship with my ex-spouse.
- I want to be treated fairly.
- I want to treat my spouse fairly.
- I want to become more stable emotionally.
- I want my spouse to become more stable emotionally.
- I want to know that I have a safety valve (insurance).
- I want to maintain a good relationship with my in-laws in the future.
- I want to maintain a good relationship with our mutual friends.
- I want to make up for the mistakes I have made.
- I want to atone for the harm I have caused.
- I want to be able to trust my ex-spouse more.
- I want my ex-spouse to be more trusting of me.
- I want to maintain sobriety (recover from addiction).
- I want my spouse to maintain sobriety (recover from addiction).
- I want to develop a better way to handle my anger/sadness/fear.
- I want my spouse to develop a better way to handle his/her anger/sadness/fear.
- I want to save the marriage.
- I want to know that we made our best effort to save the marriage.
- I want him/her to know how much s/he hurt me.
- I want him/her to apologize for what s/he has done.

- I want to do the honorable thing.
- I want to settle this matter in a way that is consistent with my religious or spiritual values.
- I want a religious annulment/Gett to void the marriage.
- I don't want him/her to live with his new girlfriend/boyfriend.
- I want to listen better.
- I want to express myself better.
- I want to be less sad (depressed).
- I want to be less angry.
- I want to be less frightened.
- I want to be less compulsive.
- I want to work on an addiction issue.
- I want closure.
- I want to be able to start healing.
- I want to be generous.
- I want my spouse to acknowledge that I have been generous.

Goals relating to the pace of the process

- I want to get done soon.
- I want to slow down the process.

APPENDIX F

Guidelines for Parents During Separation and Divorce

The following suggestions are made to help you and your children throughout the Collaborative process and beyond:

1. Think first of your children's present and future emotional and mental well-being before acting. This may be difficult, because of your own feelings, needs, and emotions, but try, try, try.

2. Maintain your own composure and good emotional balance as much as possible. In talking to yourself, verbally and in your thoughts, remember, it is not the end of the world. Laugh when you can and try to keep a sense of humor. What your children see in your attitude is, to some measure, reflected in theirs.

3. Allow yourself and your children time for readjustment. Convalescence from an emotional operation such as a dissolution of marriage is essential.

4. Remember the best parts of your marriage. Share them with your children and use them constructively.

5. Assure your children that they are not to blame for the breakup and that they are not being rejected or abandoned. Children, especially the young

children, often mistakenly feel they have done something wrong and believe that the problems in the family are the result of their own misdeeds. Small children may feel that some action or secret wish of theirs has caused the trouble between the parents. Explain to them that there are other children whose parents have been divorced and that they are not going to lose their mom or dad.

6. Continuing anger or bitterness toward your spouse can injure your children far more than the dissolution itself. The *feelings* you show often are more important than the *words* you use.

7. Refrain from voicing criticism of the other parent. It may be difficult, but it is absolutely necessary. For a child's healthy development, it is important for her or him to respect both parents.

8. Do not force or encourage your children to take sides. To do so increases frustration, guilt, and resentment.

9. Ending a marriage often leads to financial pressures on both parents. When there is a financial crisis, the parent's first impulse may be to keep the children from realizing it. Often they would rather make sacrifices themselves than ask the child to do so. Parents should carefully consider whether or not discussing financial matters with their children, in light of their age and maturity, is in their best interests.

10. Marriage breakdown is always hard on the children. They may not always show their distress or realize, at first, what this will mean to them. Parents should be direct in telling children what is happening and why, in a way a child can understand and digest. This will vary with the circumstances and with each child's age and level of understanding. The worst course is to try to hush things up and make a child feel he/she must not talk or even think about what he/she

sees is going on. Unpleasant happenings need an explanation. This explanation should be brief, prompt, direct, and honest.

11. The guilt parents may feel about the marriage breakdown may interfere in their disciplining the children. Children need consistent control, guidance, and boundaries. They also need and want to know quite clearly what is expected of them. Parents must be ready to say no when necessary.

12. Admit the fact that you are only human. You will not be able to be the perfect parent (no one ever can—in good or bad times). When you make a mistake, acknowledge it and resolve to attempt to improve day by day.

13. Understand the importance of shielding the children from the negative impact of parental conflict. If either parent becomes uncomfortable during a face-to-face or telephone discussion, rather than letting the discussion escalate into an argument, that parent should state his or her discomfort and have permission to end the discussion without further explanation. Both parents should understand that this may include hanging up the phone If It is a telephone discussion. The parent terminating the discussion should recontact the other parent within forty-eight hours to continue the discussion.

14. Read and reread these basic suggestions. Add to them by writing down your own constructive, positive approaches to the handling of your new way of living. Discuss, when practical, your thoughts and feelings with other people you trust and feel comfortable with and benefit by sharing their positive attitudes.

Bear in mind that while divorce is one of the greatest emotional stresses we can experience in our lifetimes, it also provides the greatest opportunity for those who are present to the experience to have transformational breakthroughs in personal growth.

APPENDIX G

Sample Budget

A. Housing

Rent	$_____
Mortgage (principal and interest)	$_____
Second mortgage	$_____
Real estate taxes	$_____
Home insurance	$_____
Other (specify)	$_____
_____	
SUBTOTAL	$_____

B. Utilities

Electricity	$_____
Gas/heating oil	$_____
Telephone (base and long-distance)	$_____
Water	$_____
Garbage	$_____
Other (specify)	$_____
_____	
SUBTOTAL	$_____

C. Household Operation and Maintenance

Repairs (normal/ongoing) $_____

Appliance service contracts $_____

Garden and yard work $_____

Domestic help (_____ days at $ _____ per day) $_____

Cable TV $_____

Furniture $_____

Other (specify) $_____

_____

     SUBTOTAL $_____

D. Food

Home $_____

Away $_____

_____

     SUBTOTAL $_____

E. Clothing

Clothing $_____

Shoes $_____

Laundry/dry cleaning $_____

_____

     SUBTOTAL $_____

F. Transportation

Gas and oil $_____

Auto repair and maintenance $_____

Auto licenses and stickers $_____

Auto insurance (monthly average) $_____

Auto installment payments $_____

Replacement $_____

Other (bus, taxi, parking, etc.) $_____

_____

   SUBTOTAL $_____

G. Health, Medical, Dental

Medical and hospital insurance $_____

Dental insurance $_____

Medical and health care (not covered by insurance) $_____

Dental (not covered by insurance) $_____

Medicine and drugs $_____

Life insurance (list policies and premiums) $_____

Disability insurance (list policies and premiums) $_____

Eyeglasses $_____

Orthodontist $_____

Counseling $_____

Other (specify) $_____

_____

   SUBTOTAL $_____

H. Children's Education and Child Care

Children's day care

   During school $_____

   During summer $_____

   During school vacations $_____

School tuition $_____

College tuition $_____

Room and board $_____

Books and fees $_____

Sports, lessons (specify) $_____

Children's allowance	$_____
Tutoring	$_____
School lunches	$_____
Transportation	$_____
Other (specify)	$_____
SUBTOTAL	$_____

I. Personal and Entertainment Expenses

Drugstore items	$_____
Books, magazines, newspapers	$_____
Haircuts	$_____
Cosmetics	$_____
Dues (club or professional dues not listed as a business expense)	$_____
Charities, contributions	$_____
Cultural/recreational (specify)	$_____
Entertainment	$_____
Hobbies	$_____
Other (specify)	$_____
SUBTOTAL	$_____

J. Vacations

Self	$_____
Children	$_____
Summer camp	$_____
SUBTOTAL	$_____

K. Gifts (holidays and birthdays) $_____

_____

    SUBTOTAL $_____

L. Previous Child Support $_____

_____

    SUBTOTAL $_____

M. Previous Spousal Maintenance $_____

_____

    SUBTOTAL $_____

N. Debts (list individually below)

Creditor   Balance   Monthly Payment

_____ $_____ $_____

_____ $_____ $_____

_____ $_____ $_____

    SUBTOTAL: $_____ $_____

    TOTAL OF MONTHLY EXPENSES: $_____

APPENDIX H

Ground Rules for the Client for the Collaborative Family Law Process

1. Attack the problem and concerns at hand. Do not attack each other.

2. Avoid positions; rather, express yourself in terms of needs and interests and the outcomes you would like to realize.

3. Work for what you believe is the most constructive and acceptable agreement for both of you and your family.

4. During the four-way meetings with your attorney (both attorneys and both clients are present) remember the following:

   a) Do not interrupt when the other or their attorney is speaking. You will have a full and equal opportunity to speak on every issue presented for discussion.
   b) Do not use language that blames or finds fault with the other. Use noninflammatory words. Be respectful of others.
   c) Speak for yourself; make "I" statements. Use each other's first name and avoid "he" or "she."
   d) If you share a complaint, raise it as your concern and follow it up with a constructive suggestion as to how it might be resolved.

e) If something is not working for you, please tell your attorney so your concern can be addressed.

f) List carefully and try to understand what the other is saying without being judgmental about the person or the message.

g) Talk with your attorney about anything you do not understand. Your attorney can clarify issues for you.

5. Be willing to commit the time required to meet regularly. Be prepared for each meeting.

6. Be patient—delays in the process can happen even with everyone acting in good faith.

APPENDIX I

The Importance of State of Mind in Dispute Resolution: A Spiritual Approach

THE SERENITY SPACE

There is a "space" or frame of mind in which you have available to you, moment by moment, all of the "commonsense" wisdom necessary or desirable for optimal functioning in your everyday life. I call this space the "Serenity Space." It is not some mysterious realm of consciousness only attainable after years of dedicated meditation or practice at some higher-consciousness discipline. Quite simply, this space is just your frame of reference or state of being when you are relaxed and feeling good about yourself, and not trying to "figure things out."

Close your eyes and imagine yourself at the beach (or some other place that the thought of which gives you good feelings), doing exactly what gives you the most pleasure. Stay there long enough in your imagination to experience the feelings of relaxation and peace of mind. Get in touch with the accompanying body sensations. If you can do this to any degree, then you have experienced to that degree the "Serenity Space." That's all there is to it.

It has been discovered that in the Serenity Space (or whatever you might want to call it) we all have the natural ability to tap into the collective commonsense wisdom of the universe and act, respond, and communicate in a loving, responsible, synchronous manner with what is going on in our world. It may come as a surprise to you, but our state of mind in the Serenity Space is our natural space—our birthright—the state in which we truly experience who we are.

The more time you spend in this space (and it is a choice), the brighter your world will appear. Your world will literally change over time to match your higher mood—and the better your world appears to you, the more pleasant your feelings, and the more secure your sense of well-being.

The trick to operating from the Serenity Space is not in knowing *what to do* in this positive frame of mind, but simply to keep an open mind, to trust your instincts and intuition, and to learn to stay centered in that frame of reference—without trying to figure things out.

THE INSECURITY SPACE

There is only one other possible frame of reference or "space" from which we live our lives—and, unfortunately, it is a mind-set with which we are all too familiar, many of us having spent most of our waking consciousness operating from there. I call this frame of reference the "Insecurity Space."

The Insecurity Space is the domain of the thought system of "figuring it out." Your thought system is an elaborate computerlike system consisting of all your beliefs about everything. Your thought system has gone even further and operates from the basic belief that everything in this system—all the beliefs, opinions, judgments, and so on, you have made through the years, consistent or contradictory—is essential to your survival. These "programs" are built on a fear base and have the result of drastically limiting your view of life and your ability to function in the world.

Your thought system is presided over by your ego, and the goal of the thought system is to ensure that the ego survives. It does this by assuming that everything in the world is out to "destroy" the ego and therefore everything needs to be defended against on behalf of the ego. This explains the elaborate nature of our survival programming and its ingenious design based on fear and survival.

When we operate from the Insecurity Space, we don't act—we react. We respond to everything we see in our world through our "filter" of beliefs, judgments, opinions, and so forth, that make up who we think we are. From the Insecurity Space, our filter will reflect our thought system in what we see, and this will result in the appearance of negative feelings such as anger, fear, jealousy, condemnation, mistrust, and so on. Negative behavior then follows.

Assuming that the other person with whom we are interacting is also positioned in her or her Insecurity Space, that person will then respond to our negative behavior through his or her own assortment of opinions, judgments, feelings, and behaviors that make up his or her own unique filter. We then will react to that, the other to us, and so on—creating a downward cycle of negative emotions, which all too accurately depicts many of our day-to-day "interactions."

NAVIGATING THE SPACES

In learning how to stay in the Serenity Space and out of the Insecurity Space, it may be helpful to answer the following two questions:

1. How can we recognize when we are shifting from the Serenity Space to the Insecurity Space?
2. If we find ourselves in the Insecurity Space, how can we get back to the Serenity Space?

1. *Recognizing the shift from the Serenity Space to the Insecurity Space.*
The transition from the Serenity Space to the Insecurity Space starts with a single negative thought or judgment about something, and it is usually signaled by a feeling and/or sensation of *insecurity*. Learn to key in on this feeling/sensation, and practice becoming aware of what it feels like physically for you.

Learning to recognize this feeling's onset will make it relatively easy to train yourself to shut off your negative thinking, and to choose to stay in the Serenity

Space. You don't need to avoid the circumstances in your outer world that appeared to create this emotion; just choose to stay in the Serenity Space in whatever manner works for you. With a little practice you'll develop your own tricks for responding to this "early warning" that you are about to enter the Insecurity Space.

2. *How to get from the Insecurity Space to the Serenity Space.*

Until you get some practice at early recognition of the onset of feelings of insecurity, you will probably find yourself feeling entrenched in the Insecurity Space before you are even aware that you are no longer in the Serenity Space. The more firmly enmeshed in the Insecurity Space you are, the more difficult you may find it, at first, to get back solidly into the Serenity Space.

You'll have to find what works for you to enable you to "climb out" of the machinery, so to speak. For some, the idea of "letting go," deeply felt, helps— perhaps accompanied by a deep breath of release into thoughts of a peaceful place. For others, it may be quietly meditating, or doing something physical which they find relaxing and pleasurable. Some find it helps to briefly express to each other what's going on with them—not to change the other, but to express that they are caught in their machinery.

Most importantly, however, it needs to be stressed that it is *your* thought system in which you find yourself stuck at such times, so it is *you* who must find what works for you by trial and error. Use whatever works to get yourself back to the calmness and creative wisdom available in the Serenity Space.

There is a danger in focusing on techniques for getting out of the Insecurity Space as I have been doing in the above discussion. That danger is that you may start thinking the power or "magic" is in the technique—or any technique. It is not. It needs to be stressed that no technique is really required to make the mood shift—it's just a return to your natural state. And once you experience the tremendous value of living in the Serenity Space, you learn to do it instinctively.

IMPLICATIONS FOR DISPUTE RESOLUTION

As a Collaborative lawyer, I have experienced the powerful impact that understanding the principles above can have on our ability to resolve disputes effectively.

Most of us, when we are enmeshed in disputes of any kind—and particularly marital conflicts—experience ourselves deeply caught up in the Insecurity Space. As was explained above, from that frame of reference we see the world and the other party through our negative filter and our fears. Consequently, our ability to call on our natural wisdom is severely impaired. Since the other party is also coming from his or her own Insecurity Space, a closed system of reaction, counterreaction, counter-counterreaction, and so on, is the normal interactive pattern. This context is almost always present when two parties are entering the process of dissolving their marriage. It is no wonder, then, that divorce proceedings are filled with bitterness, acrimony, and expensive legal maneuvering. Lawyers, generally as unskilled in avoiding the Insecurity Space trap as most of us, tend to get caught up in their own insecurities in attempting to meet their clients' security needs and, in addition, commonly "catch" a portion of their clients' insecurities.

Once I began to become aware of the choice I had to stay centered in the Serenity Space no matter what was going on in my world, and once I was able to convey a little of this understanding and feeling to my clients, I discovered the difference it made to both me and my clients to begin utilizing our quiet wisdom rather than to react to the other party or his/her attorney. One result was the development of a sense of perspective on the issues involved—as well as a sense of humor about it all. Functioning from the Serenity Space allows parties involved in a dispute to stay centered in a space deeper and more solid than the issues involved in the dispute. When that happens, options become available as a matter of just "knowing"—options that were not apparent or available before.

Another interesting phenomenon occurs when one (or more) parties to a dispute begin to function from the Serenity Space: It becomes catching. Coming from centered serenity and acting rather than reacting gives the other parties to the dispute room to do the same. The "loop" of reaction, counterreaction, and so on, is broken. An invitation becomes present to quiet down and begin to discover the possibilities for creative resolution of the issues in dispute based on commonsense meeting of the parties' needs. The parties develop a context for discussion based on addressing a mutual problem and seeking satisfying solutions, rather than one based on attacking each other from entrenched issue positions. The parties often discover that they are arguing over "stuff" and that neither their security nor themselves, personally, are "on the line." Wonderful, creative solutions become possible.

More importantly, the parties get some practical practice in developing their Serenity Spaces and in discovering that Serenity Spaces overlap and connect (unlike Insecurity Spaces, which cut off and separate). This learning has implications far beyond the issues that were in the dispute—implications that can alter the course of the rest of their lives.